CROYDON

The Golden Years

1900s to 1970s

First published in Great Britain by True North Books Limited

England HX3 6SN

01422 244555

www.truenorthbooks.com

The publishers would like to thank the following companies for their support in the production of this book

Boyden and Co Ltd
"Selecting tiles with style"

House of Reeves
"One of the country's leading furniture retailers"

Rawlings Opticians
"Helping Croydon with eyecare and eyewear for over 120 years"

Rowland Brothers
"Family owned and run firm since 1873"

TEXT	TONY LAX AND STEPHEN FIRTH
PHOTOGRAPHS	TONY LAX
DESIGNER	CHRIS THORPE
BUSINESS DEVELOPMENT MANAGER	JAMES GREAVES

INTRODUCTION

For all of us, memories are the currency which we use to record the changes and progress in our everyday lives and to fix our place as individuals in the greater scheme of things. The is the latest publication in our 'Memories' series of publications, covering nostalgic reflections of towns and cities throughout the UK. In this new book we will be meandering through a pictorial cross-section of life in Croydon over the last 100 years or so, to help satisfy the longing we all get from time to time, to recall memories of a different era that now seems better or simpler.

As we get older it is often easier to take a step back, and to view events and developments with a clearer sense of prospective. Our aim has been to assist in this respect by presenting a publication relevant to the area capable of rekindling memories of days gone by in an entertaining and informative manner. Looking through the pages of this book it is interesting to reflect on exactly how much change has taken place in the area over a short period, relative to its long history. Many of these photographs are unique and will inevitably remind us of experiences and events in our lives, of our families and of those whose influence and support has touched us to a greater or lesser degree.

Defining features about nostalgia are universal and can bring back fond memories from a time gone by. Recent research shows that nostalgia can counteract loneliness, boredom and anxiety. Couples feel closer and look happier when they're sharing nostalgic memories. People generally get a 'Warm Glow' inside when relating to events and occasions in the past and enjoy reminiscences about how things used to be - even when these events sometimes have a painful side. When people speak wistfully of the past, they typically become more optimistic and inspired about the future.

We can all remember events surrounding friends and family, holidays, weddings, special occasions and nights out in Croydon. So let your mind wander and think of the youthful days at the dance hall or courting in one of the many cinemas in the city. Be entertained as we take you on a sentimental journey through the pages of Croydon - The Golden Years... Happy Memories!

CONTENTS

BUILDINGS AND MONUMENTS

Above: This Fokker F.VIIA Princess Xenia, which had been used on the abortive transatlantic flight by Captain MacIntosh in 1927, is seen here landing at Croydon Airport on its return from a record-breaking flight from India to the UK on 6 September, 1928. British pilot Captain Charles Douglas Barnard and Flying Officer Eric Herbert Alliott flew the 5,000 miles in four-and-a-half days - two and a half days faster than the record set the previous year. They were accompanied on the outward journey by Mary Russell, Duchess of Bedford.

Left: We can see clearly from this photograph that it is 5pm as crowds gather for the official opening of South Norwood's clock tower, erected by the inhabitants of South Norwood to commemorate the Golden Wedding of Mr and Mrs W F Stanley, of Cumberlow, on 22 February, 1907. The clock tower is South Norwood's best known landmark, a highly decorated cast iron clock supplied by Gillet and Johnston, originally in white. In 1901, Stanley built Cumberlow Public Hall and Art Gallery and later the Stanley Technical Trade School. He was made a freeman of the borough in 1907 and died two years later in 1909. The tower in the centre of Station Road was Grade II listed in February, 1983.

In these two photographs we can get a bird's eye view of Croydon General Hospital during the early part of the 20th century. The hospital opened as a voluntary hospital in 1867 in a part of the old infirmary vacated by the workhouse, which had moved to Queens Road. It was enlarged in 1883, when the Royal Alfred Wing was built, the foundation stone having been laid by the Duke of Edinburgh. The original hospital building stood back from London Road as we can see from these images. In October, 1894, another new wing was opened by the new Archbishop of Canterbury. In the early 20th century the hospital was further extended southwards and, following a public appeal for funds initiated by the Mayor of Croydon.

It is possible the earlier of these photographs was taken around the time the King and Queen visited Croydon and its hospitals in 1916. In the main picture, crowds had gathered on the road outside the hospital as the royal party had made their way to the entrance to the hospital. The occasion was the opening of the new out-patients department and a ward extension to the south wing. The President of the Hospital, the Archbishop of Canterbury, performed the opening ceremony in June, 1927, with the King and Queen in attendance, in the presence of 200 people. Travellers on the top decks of the numerous trams passing the scene would be able to get a good view of events.

A photograph from 1912 of the spotlessly clean 18-bed children's ward at Croydon General Hospital. Doctors, nurses and some of the young patients pose for the camera. In this year, the Mayor and Mayoress opened the King Edward Memorial Wing and the extensions to the Royal Alfred Wing. In the same year x-ray, electrical and massage departments were established.

The hospital continued to serve the town until its closure in 1996. The buildings were demolished in 2004.

The Crystal Palace was a cast-iron and plate-glass structure originally built in Hyde Park to house the Great Exhibition of 1851. More than 14,000 exhibitors from around the world gathered in its 990,000 sq ft exhibition space to display examples of technology developed in the Industrial Revolution. Designed by Sir Joseph Paxton, the Great Exhibition building was 1,851 feet (564 m) long, with an interior height of 128 feet (39 m). The invention of the cast plate glass method in 1848 and its use in the Crystal Palace created a structure with the greatest area of glass ever seen in a building and astonished visitors with its clear walls and ceilings that did not require interior lights.

After the exhibition, the building was rebuilt in an enlarged form on Penge Common at the top of Penge Peak next to Sydenham Hill, an affluent south London suburb. It stood there from 1854 until its destruction by fire on 30 November, 1936. Within hours the Palace was destroyed - the glow was visible across eight counties. Even though 89 fire engines and over 400 firemen arrived they were unable to extinguish it. Reportedly, 100,000 people came to Sydenham Hill to watch the blaze, among them Winston Churchill, who said: "This is the end of an age".

The name of the famous landmark was later used to rename the nearby residential area Crystal Palace including the park that surrounds the site, which had previously been a football stadium that hosted the FA Cup Final between 1895 and 1914. Crystal Palace F.C. was founded here at the site in 1905 and played at the cup final venue in their early years.

It is hard to believe that this photograph is taken right in the heart of Croydon centre. Looking from High Street we can see the most historic buildings in Central Croydon, the former Hospital of the Holy Trinity, better known as The Whitgift Almshouses. On the corner of North End and George Street, this beautiful old building remains largely unchanged and unaffected by the relentless construction of high rise office buildings, trendy restaurants and shopping centre nearby. The Whitgift Foundation was established by John Whitgift, Archbishop of Canterbury, to provide care for the elderly and education for the young. The two foundation stones of the hospital were laid in March, 1596, and this is celebrated each year on 22 March, on Founder's Day. In 1923, after many threats of demolition from the Croydon Corporation's road-widening schemes, the now Grade I listed Almshouses, were saved by the intervention of the House of Lords.

We can see from the clocktower that it is almost 5pm when this photograph was taken of the Town Hall. This building was officially opened by Albert Edward, Prince of Wales in 1896 and following this a banquet was held in a large marquee that had been erected in the gardens. The Town Hall Gardens seen today were the creation of a late-Victorian Borough Engineer and the Victorian aspect was retained when The Queen's Gardens were planned. The original gardens were built on a site purchased as railway land when Croydon was developing. In 1889 the land was offered to Croydon Corporation for new municipal buildings and formal gardens were laid out below ground level adjacent to the Town Hall.

The gardens were renamed The Queen's Gardens when they were formally opened by Queen Elizabeth II on 21 June 1983 for the Borough Centenary, with a small plinth unveiled to commemorate the occasion. The Town Hall Gardens retain their Victorian design with carpet bedding, shrubs and lawns while the largely level Queen's Gardens have cleaner lines, laid out with lawns, flower beds and paths largely centring on a large pool and fountain.

Despite the age of this photograph, many readers will recognise this old red and cream brick building on Church Street, which still stands today. The two ladies pushing prams have just passed an early branch of Sainsbury's and are heading towards Boots Chemists, who claim to be 'Toilet Specialists' on the facia sign. In the days when few kitchens could boast a refrigerator, fresh produce to top up the larder was essential and meant regular visits to certain stores. Sainsbury's could have been one of these stores as they already had three or four similar shops around Croydon at the time. Boots was the place to go for all your medicines but also the main place to go to get your films

developed. Popular home remedies included Castor Oil - once upon a time a bottle of this vile-tasting oil was a staple in every medicine cabinet. Indian Brandee was an old remedy for digestive upsets, including bloating, wind, heartburn and constipation. While Camphorated Oil was once a popular pick-me-up. Camphor Oil was used in vapour therapy to help with respiratory disorders. Camphor was also used for inflammations, arthritis and other muscular aches and pains, rheumatism and sprains. Iodine burned like fire when applied to an open wound - this was mainly because the tincture sold for home use had an alcohol base. The skull and crossbones on the label along with the word 'poison' in capital letters probably give a clue as to why this old school remedy is rarely found in home first aid kits anymore. Cod

liver oil contains vitamin A and vitamin D and it is still used today as a supplement to help with joint problems. In the past it was regularly given to children. This was to help prevent rickets, which was very common in the early-20th Century. One brand, California Fig Syrup, was founded around 1878. They called their product "Syrup of Figs". It contained 6% alcohol and was sold at drug stores for laxative use. Fennings' Children's Cooling Powders were intended for children with mild fevers and babies experiencing teething trouble. The powder was diluted with water before use.

A single motor car leisurely makes its way up bleached white Stanhope Road, passing the elegant mansions on the left. A good run out to Epsom, Leatherhead and Box Hill was a popular jaunt for a sunny Sunday. The well-known landmark in the centre of this fantastic aerial photograph, quickly highlights we are in the Park Hill area, just to the east of Croydon town centre. Park Hill Water Tower has stood proudly in Park Hill Recreation Ground since 1867 and is one of Croydon's most recognisable buildings. Now owned by Croydon Council, the splendid Victorian building was given Grade II listed status in 1970. The structure, which is 140 ft high and 75 ft in diameter, once housed a tank with the capacity to hold 40,000 gallons of water. It has a rich history, being opened to the public as a viewing platform in 1889, giving visitors panoramic views. During the First World War the building was used as a perfect vantage point to look out for Zeppelin raids but a rapid increase of houses in the vicinity caused water supply problems which meant the end of the water tower's working life. Surrounding the tower is Park Hill Recreation Ground. It runs from Barclay Road to Coombe Road beside the railway line. At the southern end, at the very top of the hill which forms the park, it joins the grounds of Coombe Cliff once the home of members of the Horniman Tea family. In 1930, just after this photograph was taken, Croydon Corporation purchased Horniman's House, Coombe Ciff, as a convalescent home for children. In 1960, after a number of uses, it became an adult education centre. Park Hill Recreation Ground and Coombe Cliff Garden were renamed Park Hill in 1964.

Left: Traffic is queuing outside the old Central Post Office in Croydon in this image from the summer of 1939. The gent in this sporty two-seater, possibly an Austin 7 Seven Mulliner, is taking advantage of the sunny conditions. The outlook would be much gloomier in a few months time after the onset of WWII and wartime petrol rationing, introduced on 22 September, that year. To the right of the Post Office is Rawling & Oldfield and, next door, Hope Brothers gents outfitters. Rawling is a name synonymous with options in Croydon, as Alfred John Rawling opened his first shop at 137b North End, Croydon as far back as 18 September, 1895. He moved to these premises on High Street in 1914. Remarkably, the fine Post Office building has survived road widening and development schemes and even the opening of a large new post office next to East Croydon station in the 1970s.

Above: This was one of a number of housing estates built between the wars. Croydon's busy airport and its excellent road and rail connections with the inner city, encouraged the housing boom in this area of London. This photograph shows the partly built Waddon housing estate, after the older squalid properties had been swept away. The view of Denning Avenue takes in the recreation ground to Duppas Hill. Within a few months, new residents would move in and have the benefit of hot water on tap and the first opportunity to get into a proper bath in the privacy of their own bathroom. Things that we take for granted today would have been a luxury at this time. In the inter-war years Waddon had the most Croydon Corporation owned homes in Croydon with 1,125 council houses and 80 council flats. Waddon has a long history of industrial trades. The Croydon gasworks was built on Waddon Marsh in 1867. An electricity generating station opened in 1896. The opening of the Purley Way in 1925 prompted the building of a number of factories including for Redwing Aircraft Ltd, Tizer Ltd, Standard Steel Co and Metal Propellers Ltd to name but a few. Croydon Corporation built the Waddon pumping station in 1910–11 on the road now called Waddon Way.

The Greyhound Restaurant in Park Lane was an impressive establishment when this photograph was taken in the 1930s and it was to remain a favourite eating house with many locals until it closed in 1959. In 1926 the old inn underwent major alterations to its extensive premises and excellent stabling facilities and during the work builders uncovered an inscription which dated from Tudor times. In the 17th century it is reported that some of Fairfax's soldiers put up in 'The Greyhound' during the Civil War. Sherlock Holmes writer Sir Arthur Conan Doyle also stayed here in the early part of the 20th century. By November, 1959, this splendid building had also disappeared, as we can see from the clouds of dust created during the demolition. One the dust had settled a clear view of the town hall from this prospective was a rare sight. Eventually the St George's Walk Shopping Precinct was to stand on the site of the old Greyhound.

Below: Road works are in progress on Church Street outside Croydon Parish Church when this photograph was taken in the 1950s. We can still see the trolleybus wire cables in the sky above the church. Miles and miles of this cable and points called a 'frog', hung over our streets for decades and we gave little thought to it. Croydon Parish Church has a long and distinguished history and, together with the manor house nearby, which is now Old Palace School, is the oldest foundation in the town. Six former Archbishops of Canterbury lie buried within it. Some of the country's most famous monarchs, including Henry VII and VIII and Elizabeth I visited and stayed here. It is believed to have been founded in Saxon times since there is a record of "a priest of Croydon" in 960, although the first record of a church building is in Domesday Book (1086). The church has had close links with the Archbishops of Canterbury who had a palace in Croydon.

Right: This is a fabulous picture of a dad with his two young children near the iconic pumping station off Surrey Street, on a summer's day in July, 1951. The impressive pumping station was constructed in neo Gothic style, built in four phases from 1851 and completed in 1866. These tots could be classed as baby boomers after an explosion in the birth rate in the late 1940s and 1950s. World War II was a long and difficult conflict. Peace in 1945 came as an immense relief and people celebrated by embarking upon relationships that had been postponed because of the fighting. The result was a sharp rise in births during the post-war years - the so-called Baby Boom. Despite a loving family, these two kids would still have to suffer from rationing of food and clothes. The girl's frock and dungarees on the boy could well have been hand-me-downs or home-made. It was quite normal to go without the sweets, biscuits, crisps and fizzy drinks that would be taken for granted by future generations. Before sweet rationing ended in February, 1953, the most prized thing in your Christmas stocking would have been a small, two-ounce bar of chocolate. The Victorian water pumping station, now no longer in use, is a Grade II listed building. Constructed in neo-Gothic style, the impressive building was built in four phases from 1851 and completed in 1866. The view of the historic pumping station building is still the same today, however, it is now surrounded by modern high rise structures.

Work was still taking place on the perimeter of Croydon B Power Station when this photograph was taken in March 1952, almost two years after the opening. A workman pushing a wheelbarrow is making his way towards the temporary gable to the turbine and boiler house at the northerly end of the station. Work first started on the site in 1939, but was suspended during World War II, starting again in 1945. It was eventually completed in 1950 and the plant was fully operational by the end of the following year. The power station was designed by Robert Atkinson and built by Sir Robert McAlpine & Sons. It was decommissioned in 1984 and in a disused state was used in the filming of parts of Terry Gilliam's 1985 film Brazil. The station was demolished in 1991 and an IKEA store was opened on the site. Two large chimneys were retained and remain a local landmark.

Fairfield Halls has been at the centre of Croydon life for over 50 years. Since the Queen Mother opened the building on 2 November, 1962, some of the greatest stars of music, variety, comedy, opera and theatre have graced Fairfield's stages and it is a venue of national and cultural importance.

For many centuries, from early Tudor times, the 'Fair Field' land in this photograph was used for 'Fairs', which were held every year. The ground was also used for gravel extraction, and between 1930 and 1960 the land was home to both a car park and also air raid shelters during WWII.

In this fabulous aerial view, we can see the completed halls prior to the opening, while work is still being carried out on what was to become Fairfield Gardens and underground car park to the left of the main building. Off Park Road to the left, is the new Croydon College of Technology. On the right, running parallel with Barclay Road, is the Arnhem Gallery, named after Croydon's twin town in the Netherlands. Further along the road where all the cars are parked is now the Croydon Magistrates Court building.

ENTERTAINMENT AND EVENTS

This fabulous image from the Edwardian era is of the grand Swan and Sugarloaf Hotel building in South Croydon. A destination for London's buses for many years, we can see an unique line up of General London General Omnibus Company (LOGC) omnibuses outside the pub. The LGOC was the principal bus operator in London between 1855 and 1933. The current Swan and Sugarloaf building on the junction of Selsdon Road and Brighton Road, was built in 1896 and it had stables for tram horses at the back. One theory for the unusual name is said to be the result of a misunderstanding of the coat of arms of the Archbishop of Canterbury, which shows a mitre, shaped like a loaf of sugar, and a crosier, which is shaped like a swan's neck. During the Edwardian era women wore a very tight corset, or bodice, and dressed in long skirts. For men, top hats remained a requirement for upper class formal wear while soft felt Homburgs or stiff bowler hats were worn with lounge or sack suits. The pub continued to provide a service to the local community for over 100 years until its closure in March, 2010.

The Royal Silver Jubilee year created, if only temporarily, a buoyant mood in the country. King George V and Queen Mary were popular figures and for a brief spell there was a carnival atmosphere across the nation and a renewed optimism. Circuses of all sizes flourished, not just the 'big names' such as Billy Smart, Bertram Mills and Sanger. During the Jubilee year there seemed to be a circus on every corner and each one had a way of promoting the event. Here we can see an elephant from Sanger's Circus taking a publicity stroll in North End on 16 July, 1935. Typically for the British summer, the rain is pouring down and the elephant's miniature pony companion looks like he is trying to shelter from the inclement weather. Handlers had to be very careful as animals occasionally attacked attendants and this chap seems to have his hands full with two animals to look after on the main road. The Croydon public did not seem to mind, however, as a small crowd had stopped to watch proceedings.

Remembrance is part of modern British life, culture and heritage. It becomes a particular feature of the public calendar each year when public, private, formal and informal Remembrance events take place throughout the UK. Each year at the eleventh hour of the eleventh day of the eleventh month, we observe a two minutes silence. Armistice Day on 11 November marks the end of the First World War and is a day to remember and honour those who have

paid the price for our freedom. In this photograph from 1926, massive Croydonian crowds had gathered out of respect for those whose lives were prematurely ended by conflict in the Great War.

The war memorial stands outside the Library on Katharine Street in central Croydon and has the inscription: 'A tribute to the men and women of Croydon who died and suffered'. It was unveiled on 22 October,

1921, as we can see the ceremony that took place, in the other two photographs taken at the time. It was paid for by a public subscription organised by the Borough of Croydon. It is of particular note for the balance struck between military and domestic suffering.

Here we have two contrasting views of Katherine Street, taken approximately 20 years apart. In the first scene outside the town hall, we can see that crowds had turned out in force to get a glimpse of the future King of England. Crowds cheered as the Royal motorcade travelled in procession along the street towards the reception party. Banners across the street welcomed H.R.H. Prince George during the Incorporation Golden Jubilee celebrations on 9 June, 1933.

Every vantage point was being used, including the rooftops and one man has even climbed on top of the canopy over the entrance to The Kings Arms Hotel. During his visit, Prince George, Duke of Kent, also laid a foundation stone for the extension to the General Hospital.

Some 20 years later, things are a little quieter. The people of Croydon were going about their normal daily routines on a bright, sunny day. On the south side of the street is the town hall. This is Croydon's third town hall and dates from 1896. A statue of Queen Victoria gazes north, under the watchful eye of John Whitgift. His statue is built into the library wall, close to sculpted

friezes that proclaim: 'health, study, religion, recreation and music'. Across the road we can see the Kings Arms Hotel which was first mentioned in records in 1674. The building was demolished in 1963. Next door is The Croydon Hotel, which stood on the corner of Katherine Street and High Street. Sadly, the buildings on this side of the street have gone completely to be replaced by 1960s characterless, mainly glass buildings.

earchlights from the town hall clock tower cut through the night sky like a beacon. They shone out brightly in all directions to illuminate the 50th anniversary celebrations of Croydon's incorporation as a borough. Thousands of light bulbs combined to make celebratory arches and a fitting display for this momentous day. The occasion was marked by a royal visit, when Prince George came to town to share in the fun and festivities.

The banner above Kennards, North End, says, 'For 75 years Kennards has led the commerce of the town'. Kennards was a truly magical department store in Croydon and was using the opportunity of a Royal visit to promote their contribution to the town since the stores opening in 1853. Prince George (the fourth son of King George V and Queen Mary) had been invited by the local Chamber of Commerce to lay the foundation stone of the new wing at the General Hospital, at the same time as the celebrations were to take place to mark the 50 years Croydon had been a Borough. The town was bedecked with flags and bunting as we can clearly see in this photograph from June 1933. Kennards was one of the first UK businesses to use publicity to sell its goods. In the 1920s they introduced pony rides for children in store, at the Frith Road end. The success of this was followed by opening of a small zoo. This originally hosted some monkeys, a camel, a peacock, some birds and other small animals. This attracted lots of children with their parents, so they decided to expand the zoo further with more exotic animals. In 1930 two lions were introduced, along with a hyena and a porcupine. The zoo closed in 1939 with the outbreak of the Second World War.

All eyes are on this young woman as she prepares to take the plunge into the cold water at the Purley Way Lido in September, 1937. This was only a couple of years after the ozone pool was officially opened by His Worship the Mayor, Alderman J. Trumble. U.S.A. Olympic Diving Champions Messrs Pete Desjardins and Harold "Dutch" Smith gave a diving display on the day, to stun and thrill the crowds at the unique lido. At the height of its popularity, it attracted 9,000 visitors a day during the summer with the diving boards of three, five and ten metres the main attraction. Quite surprisingly the boards are now among Croydon's list of listed buildings, being given Grade II listed status by English Heritage on 21 March, 2013. Largely due to the dwindling number of bathers, because of cheap package holidays abroad, the pool closed for good in 1979. Two years later a garden centre opened on the site but the diving stage remained, bedecked with plants and flowers. From the high board, looking across Purley Way, we can see the famous Croydon Airport in the background.

The two youngsters representing the King and Queen don't look too happy in this photograph from St Jude's Church Hall, on 12 May, 1937. Patriotic Croydon families had gathered together to celebrate the coronation of George VI. The hall had been decked out with streamers, bunting and union flags for the benefit of residents, old and young, in the Thornton Road area. The community rallied round to produce a fabulous spread of sandwiches and cakes, with jelly and ice cream for the kids. The party would no doubt include games of charades, pin the tail on the donkey, blind man's bluff and musical chairs. It was a fun day that was a long time coming. The king's father had died 16 months earlier. In the meantime there had been the proclamation of Edward VIII and his abdication just before Christmas. He remains the only British monarch to have voluntarily renounced the throne since the Anglo-Saxon period. He was succeeded by Albert, who took the regal name of George VI, despite a certain amount of trepidation.

Left: The Grand Theatre, Croydon, was built by Brough in 1896 and was opened in April that year. A prominent sign above the canopy of the theatre tells us that seats for their twice nightly variety shows have 'popular prices'. The photograph was taken in the 1930s, advertising the variety show. The popularity of variety was beginning to dwindle with the advent of the talking pictures. By the 1930s many theatres had closed or become cinemas. Other forms of entertainment, such as revue, had become popular and many variety performers made their names through radio, film and later, television. In the 1930s and 40s artists such as Ted Ray, Tommy Trinder, Gracie Fields, Will Hay, George Formby, Sandy Powell and Max Miller appeared regularly in variety up and down the country. The Grand closed in the early part of the war when Croydon was extensively bombed, but reopened in the latter part of 1942. The theatre closed in April, 1959, after entertaining audiences for a total of 63 years and despite a petition signed by 100,000 people who had battled to save it the theatre was demolished and an office block and shops were built on the site.

Below and Right: The Scala Cinema originally opened in 1914. World War I was in progress at the time, and the cinema's staff were taken from those who were exempt from military service. In 1921, an 11-year-old local schoolboy named David Lean made the Scala his first ever cinema visit, when he saw 'The Hound of the Baskervilles'. He later became one of the UK's most famous film directors. In the 1920s, Allder's Department Store was built around the Scala Cinema, and the facade was rebuilt to blend into the store's façade, as we can see in the photograph (right) from 1926. After the WWII the 880-seat Scala went into decline and a sudden decision was made to close the cinema in 2 March, 1952.

Right: The Empire Theatre of Varieties opened in May 1906 on the site of the former Palace Theatre of Varieties. Designed by Sprague, it cost £30,000 to build and was constructed by Walter Wallis. The new theatre had a narrow frontage to the street and a 75 foot high ornamental tower with figures by Arrowsmith, a local sculptor. On going through the entrance a corridor and stairs lead to the foyer space which gave access to the grand circle and boxes. The auditorium was on three levels – stalls, grand circle and gallery – seating up to 2,500 people. The auditorium's original colour scheme was cream, gold and white with red furnishings and it had a domed roof with a stained glass roof light. An orchestra pit could accommodate 14 musicians. The building operated as both a theatre and a cinema for over 50 years. It closed as a cinema on 30 May 1959, and was demolished two years later to make way for an office block, car park and shops.

Below: Located in the southeast London district of South Norwood. Built for the Oscar Deutsch chain of Odeon Theatres Ltd. The Odeon South Norwood opened on 26 July, 1937 with Hazel Ascot in "Talking Feet", with Hazel Ascot appearing in person. The exterior had a cream tile cladding, with several horizontal bands of jade green Vitrolite tiles. There was a central window above the entrance, which had decorative grille work. Inside the auditorium, seating was provided for 1,020 in the stalls and 552 in the circle. The Odeon was closed by the Rank Organisation on 20 February, 1971 with Sydney Poitier in "They Call Me Mister Tibbs" and Rock Hudson in "Hornet's Nest". It was purchased by a redevelopment company and was demolished. By 2006 a supermarket had been built on the site.

A WH Cullen groceries and provisions van is parked outside the Davis Theatre in this photograph from 1958. The No12 bus to South Croydon Village is just passing a group of people waiting at the bus stop on High Street. When it was built in 1928, the Davis Theatre was the second largest cinema to be built in the UK and the largest cinema in England, with more than 3,700 seats, a ballroom, café and royal circle with luxurious armchair seats. Many live shows were performed at the Davis Theatre, highlights being two performances of the London Philharmonic Orchestra, conducted by Sir Thomas Beecham in January and October 1939. Jeannette MacDonald gave a sell-out concert on 7th July 1946, with other concerts by Maurice Chevalier, Frankie Laine, Gracie Fields, Liberace, Bill Haley and the Comets, Paul Anka and Mario Lanza in 1958. With the downturn in cinema-going and the introduction of commercial television, the announcement came in December 1958 that the Davis Theatre would be closing. Some older readers might remember seeing 'Rally Round the Flag, Boys' and 'The Lavender Hill Mob', being screened at the time of the photograph, which was taken not long before the cinema closed. The Davis Theatre was demolished in late-1959, and an office block named Davis House and car parking space was built on the site. This was a great loss to the people of Croydon.

Even after the end of World War II there were still casualties. In this startling photograph we can see the wreckage of an R.A.F. Transport Command Dakota aircraft, which got into difficulties. Flying low just after it had left Croydon, the aircraft crashed behind a row of houses in Mitchley Avenue, near the Purley Downs golf course. One eye-witness said he heard the engines spluttering and then picking up for a brief noisy burst. It suddenly swooped down in a nose dive and crashed. The nose was partly buried in the ground and the tail was leaning against the front roof of a cottage. Sadly, four of the crew of seven were killed. Three Canadian soldiers were taken to hospital.

Policemen keep the enthusiastic crowd back as the Thanksgiving parade of troops and auxiliary units march through the Croydon streets. We had become used to morale-boosting parades throughout the war - this one, however, was different. It was a victory parade in May, 1945, and the marchers had a spring in their step. Every service and organisation formed part of the mile-long procession. Following the band of the London Fire Service were representatives of the Royal Artillery, the Scots Guards, the RAF, the Home Guard and the Women's Auxiliaries and Civil Defence workers. In this photograph we can see volunteers from the Red Cross in traditional uniform and white gloves, marching past Croydon Town Hall. Throughout the Second World War the Red Cross carried out extensive services for the sick and wounded for prisoners of war and for civilians needing relief as a result of enemy action. Today, however, was a celebration and it was time to let down your hair and party.

It's 75 years since Winston Churchill launched his 'V for Victory' campaign and led Britain to a victory over Nazi Germany. Known for his rousing speeches and bulldog scowl, Churchill was a brilliant statesman and his legacy remains stronger than ever. In this photograph, taken post war on 9 March, 1948, he is cheered as he arrives in North Croydon, to show his support for the Conservative candidate in the by-election.

Churchill toured the constituency, making speeches from the top of his car, through crowded streets and speaking into microphones at various points. He was supporting F.W.Harris, a local businessman, in the hotly contested North Croydon seat. Helpfully, his daughter, Mary Soames, was then in a Croydon maternity hospital giving birth to her son, Nicholas, bringing the campaign positive publicity. In the end, Harris triumphed with an 11,664 majority. A national newspaper the next morning ran the headline "Oh what a beautiful morning". The song (from Oklahoma!) became his theme tune when touring Croydon.

Above: George VI died on 6 February, 1952 at Sandringham and was buried at St George's Chapel, Windsor Castle, on 15 February, 1952, following a State Funeral in the Chapel. The people of Croydon played their part in the nations day of grief. A respectful crowd of several thousand gathered outside the town hall, near the war memorial, on Katherine Street to pay their last respects. Traffic came to a standstill as two minutes silence was observed. All the men in the crowd doffed their hats and the women bowed their heads. Big Ben chimed 56 times, one for every year of his short life. In Croydon there were mixed emotions. His daughter, HRH The Princess Elizabeth, had been proclaimed Queen Elizabeth II on 8 February, 1952. We were saddened by the loss of our monarch, but his passing heralded a new era. A young and vibrant Queen was on the throne.

Right: Trolleybuses served the London Passenger Transport Area for just over 30 years in the mid-20th century. For much of its existence, the London system was the largest in the world. It had 68 routes, and a maximum fleet of 1811 trolleybuses. Barely 30 years after its inception, London's large fleet of electric buses was withdrawn. The first 60 trolleybuses were operated by London United Tramways (LUT), from a depot at Fulwell in south-west London. They were nicknamed "Diddlers" and first ran on 16 May, 1931, Croydon's trolleybuses were Routes 630 and 654, with a common stretch of overhead wiring along Tamworth Road into Station Road, West Croydon. The trolleybus replaced former tram routes in the mid 1930s but were themselves ousted by the diesel bus in two stages in March, 1959, and July, 1960. In 1954, it was announced that all trolleybuses were to be replaced with the exception of the post-war vehicles, which would be retained until about 1970 and run over the original LUT routes. Conversion began in 1959, using RT buses for the first three stages and new Routemasters for the remainder.

Above: This photograph looks to have been taken much earlier than it actually was. At first glance it could be the Civil Defence Corps attending a bombed out building during the Second World War. It is, in fact, a training exercise a decade after the final shots had been fired. Even by 1955 people were still not confident that lasting peace had been achieved and so the Civil Defence Corps mounted practice sessions to show how they would respond. The Croydon Division often used the derelict buildings on South Norwood Sewage Farm as a focus for their training sessions. This exercise was to show off the Division's state of preparation and its co-operation with other uniformed services, such as the fire and ambulance crews. Rubble from war damaged buildings eventually mounted up in this area to form what is now the large hill behind the sports arena today. It is the principal viewpoint in South Norwood Country Park.

British-American actor, Peter Mayhew, for a long time lived in South Croydon and always gained attention when he walked through the local shopping mall. The gentle giant (7ft 3ins tall), can be seen here in his doorway in May 1980, with Mirror showbiz editor Gordon Blair. Before Star Wars, Mayhew worked primarily as a hospital orderly in London. He along with his fellow Star Wars actor David Prowse both have an association with Croydon. Prowse, aka the Dark Lord, Darth Vader, was born in Bristol and now lives in Addiscombe, where he has resided for over 50 years. When casting for the first Star Wars film in 1976, producer George Lucas had in mind bodybuilder Prowse for the role of hairy 'Wookiee' warrior, Chewbacca, but instead Prowse chose to play Darth Vader and the role went to Mayhew. Both actors played their respective characters for the entirety of the original Star Wars trilogy.

Left and right: How fantastic is this photograph (left) of the Her Majesty Queen Elizabeth The Queen Mother, smiling as she receives flowers from this very smartly dressed young boy at the official opening of Fairfield Halls in November, 1962. The prestigious venue which also includes Ashcroft Theatre, named after Croydon born actress Dame Peggy Ashcroft, went on to host some of the greatest stars of music, variety, comedy, opera, at the world-renowned venue.

In the picture, below, we can see crowds of local Croydon folk waiting patiently outside the new building in anticipation of the arrival of the Queen Mum, on that special day in 1962. The Queen Mother held an unshakeable place in British affections for more than half a century and the people of Croydon had come out in force to catch a glimpse of her from behind the barriers.

Right: All the girls with union flags in hand, are on their best behavior as Queen Elizabeth II walks past on the red carpet at the Old Palace School on 2 November, 1960. The Sisters of Mercy are escorting the Royal couple, with Prince Philip in the background stopping to have a chat with some of the assembled dignitaries. The flowers had been presented to the Queen by Head Girl, Pam Gill. Her Majesty and His Royal Highness visited for a short stay with tea and a performance by the girls of the 'Old Palace Pageant.' Earlier, crowds of cheering well-wishers had lined the streets of Croydon to get a glimpse of the Royal couple as they passed. Celebrations were taking place as part of Croydon's Millenary Year.

FAIRFIELD HALLS
in the FAIRFIELD
HALL CROYDON

5.30 | THURSDAY, 25th APRIL | 8.00
TWO CONCERTS

JOHN SMITH presents
MERSEY BEAT SHOW CASE

Featuring

The Beatles
"Please please me"

GERRY & THE PACEMAKERS | THE BIG THREE
"How do you do it"

BILLY KRAMER & THE DAKOTAS | VIC SUTCLIFFE
Compere

GUEST STAR

John Leyton
"Cupboard Love" etc., etc.,

The images on these two pages have kindly been provided by John Spring from Fairfield Halls and give us a brief nostalgic reminder of the star names who were appearing at the venue in the 'Swinging Sixties' and into the 1970s.

As we can see from the poster on the left, the Beatles played the brand new Fairfield Halls on 25 April, 1963. This was part of the 'Mersey Beat' mini tour, one month after the release of their first album 'Please Please Me'. Also on the bill were Gerry and the Pacemakers, The Big Three and Billy J.Kramer and the Dakotas. The event was organised by promoter John Smith, who had arranged for singer John Leyton to headline the concert. On the day, however, Leyton was ill and cancelled his appearance, leaving The Beatles to take their place at the top of the bill.

In contrast to scenes only a few months later when girl fans would be screaming in the aisles and crying hysterically as Beatlemania took its grip, the crowd of female fans waiting outside for the April concert were quite small in number as can be seen in the photograph below. Once inside they seemed very reserved, sitting politely with legs crossed. This would change dramatically when the Beatles returned to Fairfield on 7 September, 1963.

During this era, Fairfield Halls was attracting some of the biggest entertainment acts in the world. It is inconceivable that today's big names would play live, at relatively small venues compared to today's standards, but 1960s pop royalty such as, the Beatles, Cliff Richard and the Rolling Stones did and for the unbelievable equivalent today of between 25p (5/-) to 52p (10/6) per ticket. In the rare photograph above, we can see the Rolling Stones lined up backstage at Fairfield Halls on Sunday, 12 April, 1964. Left to right are; Mick Jagger, Brian Jones, Bill Wyman, Keith Richards and drummer Charlie Watts. The 'All Star Package Show' featured The Barracudas, The Worryin' Kind, Dave Dee (later of Dave Dee, Dozy, Beaky, Mick and Tich) and his group the Bostons. The line-up also featured country-rock band The Overlanders, who had a massive hit in 1966 with their version of "Michelle" and Germany's leading recording group, The Rattles.

Home entertainment in the early 1960s consisted of just two television channels, both broadcasting in black and white. BBC2 didn't arrive until 1964, with colour programmes following three years later. When Fairfield Halls came along in 1962, it was able to offer a wide variety of live entertainment for all the family. It became a major venue for professional music, plays, musicals, stand-up comedy and classical music and a significant proportion of Fairfield's programme was also for community events. It has been used by local schools as the venue for their annual choral concerts, as well as being regularly used by local music, opera, amateur dramatic and religious organisations. In the picture on the right, we can see children being children, making faces as they pose for a photograph taken at Fairfield Halls in the 70s.

THE STREETS OF CROYDON

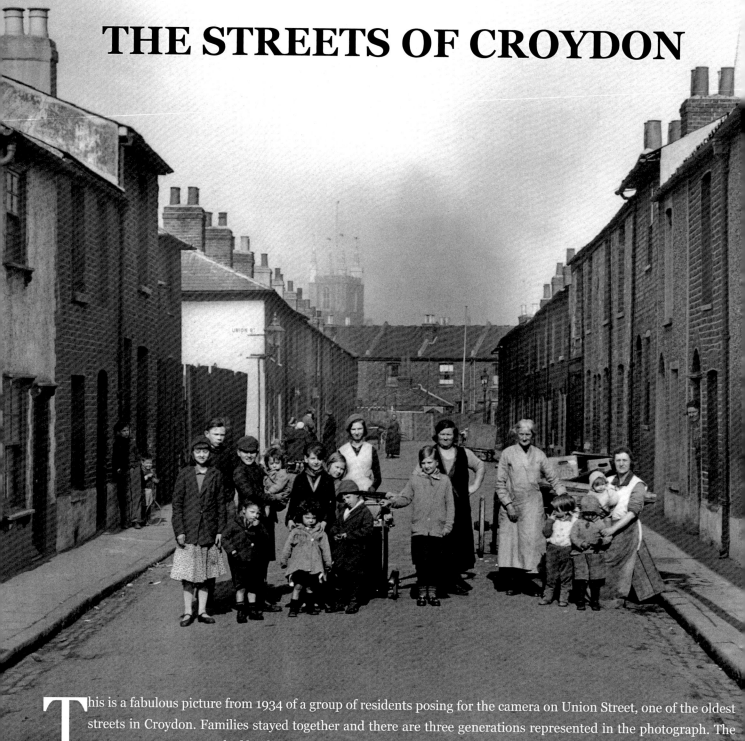

This is a fabulous picture from 1934 of a group of residents posing for the camera on Union Street, one of the oldest streets in Croydon. Families stayed together and there are three generations represented in the photograph. The 1930s economy was marked by the effects of the great depression. This led to higher unemployment and widespread poverty. This street was typical of the maze of little streets full of terraced houses, with front doors that opened directly onto the pavement. Victorian housing stock was often in very poor repair, had inadequate sanitation and homes were often over-crowded. However, camaraderie and the spirit of friendship tended to be very strong between neighbours and this led to an unshakeable community spirit. Unlike today, kids were able to play out on the streets as there were no problems with cars or lorries, just the occasional horse and cart. The street was eventually demolished in the 1970s and rebuilt and modernised, although the layout still roughly exists.

Lunchtime traffic queues at the traffic lights along George Street, at the junction with Park Lane and Wellesley Road. A car is struggling to join the main flow alongside J. & T. Robinson Ltd. Some keen fishermen may remember that Ogden Smith used to run a business selling fishing tackle from the shop above Robinson's. The Public Hall near to to East Croydon Railway Station, was located on the north east corner of George Street and Wellesley Road. It was built with a library and scientific instution use, and was converted into a full time cinema on 16th May 1910. Seating capacity had been slightly increased from the original 531 in the stalls and 116 in the balcony. It had previously screened films occasionally from around 1906. The Public Hall's use as a full time cinema was short lived as it closed by the end of 1910, although occassional film performances were held there until 1920, as it retained its Cinematograph Licence. After World War II, the building was demolished and a parade of shops and a Barclays Bank was built on the site. This picture from the late 1940s shows a route 12 post-war RT class in original condition dating from about 1948. These buildings were the Public Halls on the corner of Wellesley Road. Further along the road is East Croydon Station.

From the clock on the outside of the Lloyds Bank building we can see it is 12.40 pm and Croydon High Street is busy with shoppers, mostly unaware they are being caught on camera. The old Ford travelling towards the camera and the lack of road markings, tend to give the impression this photograph is older than it actually is. The clothing and fashion along with the AEC Regent III RT double-decker in the background, suggest that the image is actually from the early 1950s. This photograph is taken looking northwards towards George Street and Crown Hill crossroads. Older readers may also have spotted the cone-shaped tower which once topped the Burtons Tailor and Milletts building. Not many of us, however, will remember the building as The Crown, one of the oldest hostelries in Croydon. The Crown was offering rooms and stabling as long ago as the 14th century. It closed around 1940 and a menswear business took over until the redevelopment of the town centre.

The second image is taken from just further along High Street, looking back in the opposite direction. Burtons again features on the right, but how many readers can remember the Black and White milk bar in North End. At the time, Milk Bars had become a common sight in virtually every high street and Croydon was no exception. In the beginning people laughed at the idea of selling milk in London. Back in the 1930s, the number of Black and White Milk

Bars, controlled by Hugh D. McIntosh, grew rapidly. By the time this photograph was taken however, coffee bars were taking over and the milk bar days were numbered. By 1953 new style coffee bars sprang up all over London, with Formica tables and lino floors. The first was The Moka espresso bar at 29 Frith Street. Opened by Gina Lollabrigida, it became the model for many classic Formica cafes to come.

The vintage Austin car pulls away as the No42 Thornton Heath tram trundles down the centre of the road in the third of our pictures of High Street. Apart from the Whitgift Almshouses on the right at the junction with George Street, the landscape has changed completely in this view today. There is little comparison to the pedestrianised and traffic restricted area we see today at the entrance to North End. The tram tracks along the High Street have long gone, but since the introduction of the Tramlink system serving Croydon and surrounding areas in 2000, there is a tram line running along from Crown Hill to George Street, from left to right in this photograph.

This is a great picture to give us a feel for Croydon life pre WWII. The fashion was very smart and glamourous, as this was the era of the big bands and dancing. Hollywood and the movies also began to be very influential as people wanted to wear the styles they had seen on the screen. This photograph was taken in the summer of 1938 looking down Crown Hill in a happier time as people went about their daily business unaware of the horrors that were just around the corner. The advertising hoarding is promoting a great August Bank Holiday open-air event at Crystal Palace, despite the fact that the Palace itself had been destroyed by fire less than two years before. We can also see from the clock outside James Walker watches that is just before noon. Today, this section has been pedestrianised and it is unusual for most of us to see two-way traffic on the hill. Traffic coming up Crown Hill would have to turn right on Middle Street. Only the single line tram link would use this section of road where we see the vintage Packard 8 coming towards the camera.

Right: In this photograph we can just see the entrance to Surrey Street, home to the oldest known street market in all of Britain. Surrey Street Market has traded since 1236. In 1922 the Croydon Corporation took over the market and established it as a daily market (except Sunday). Further development of the land led to the building of the Grants Entertainment Centre which effectively dominates the old market triangle of land. Consequently the street trading activity all moved to Surrey Street. On the right we can see a sign for the upper floor billiards hall. Billiards first started to become popular in modern culture once billiard halls and pool rooms were created. Men would gather at these halls to smoke their pipes, wager on the games, drink liquor and reminisce about their lives.

Below: The Fabric House clock tells us it is mid morning, just after 10.30am. A classic Leyland-built RT London bus makes its way along North End in this fabulous street scene from the 1950s. Although there are still tram tracks, the retirement programme started in October 1950 and London's last trams ran in the early hours of 6 July, 1952. In the distance we can see the massive S & O sign for the Stockwell & Oxford store, which sold quality furniture and glassware, among other things. Opposite is the Empire Theatre, which during this period was to change from a live theatre to The Eros Cinema. Personal service was a byword in these times and stores employed delivery boys to convey goods directly to your door. Two examples can be seen on the right hand side of the image althought an old pram is probably not the best way to transport his produce!

Right: This is a fantastic old photograph of George Street, probably dating from the very beginning of the Edwardian period. The street is a throng with elegantly dressed ladies and gentlemen going about their daily business. On the roads the horse was king and still the main form of private and road transport in Britain. London needed some 300,000 horses to keep it moving. The

majority were used by cabmen, the others worked for traders like laundrymen, grocers or rag-and-bone men. Change was on the horizon however and we can see in the distance one of the first electric trams. The electric tram took some decades to establish itself in London. It was not until 1901 that Croydon Corporation introduced the first fully operational electric tram services in the Greater London area, using power delivered from overhead wires.

George Street was once one of the premier shopping streets in Croydon. In the photograph we can see it is lunchtime from the clock on the old Thrift Warehouse and that it is a sunny day, judged by the number of awnings in place on the right hand side of the street only. It was commonplace for the ladies to meet and gossip in the little tea shops and for the men to get their moustaches waxed at the barber's shop. High class milliners had fine hats on display from the latest Paris fashions. Middle class ladies had their own private accounts with dressmakers, as buying off-the-peg clothing was not their style.

Right: Croydon's Public Hall on George Street, as it was almost 70 years ago, not long after the end of WWII. Samuel Coleridge-Taylor's name is often linked to the venue as on a number of occasions he conducted music at the hall. This view of the north east corner of George Street and Wellesley Road, has changed out of all recognition today.

The Public Hall was located near to East Croydon Railway Station. It was built with a library and scientific

institution use and was converted into a full time cinema on 16 May, 1910. The Hall's use as a full time cinema was short lived as it closed by the end of the year, although occasional film performances were held there until 1920.

After World War II, the building was demolished and a parade of shops and a Barclays Bank was built on the site.

Above: The well established firm of J. & T. Robinson can be seen on the corner. Older readers who visited the shop with their parents, may well remember the owner Jack Pomper. Mums flocked to the store to sign up for the latest kitchen appliances. Washday red hands became a thing of the past with the new electric washing machine. Upright and cylinder vacuum cleaners helped to take some of the drudgery out of daily housework. Mr Pomper, was being very bold with his promotional advertising, suggesting he had the largest selection of appliances in Surrey. The town was to change dramatically in the late 1950s and 1960s and the buildings in this photograph would not survive the march of progress. They would be demolished as part of the town centre improvements.

Right: This is an elevated photograph looking along the length of George Street, with the almshouses on the left. George Street was once the premier shopping street in Croydon. Butchers hung game outside their shops, and the smell of freshly baked bread wafted past our nostrils. There were little tea shops where elegant ladies could meet and gossip about events in their social circle. Men had their moustaches waxed at the barber's shop and high class milliners had fine hats on display. Everything was made to measure in tailors that would know their customers by name. The view at the far end of George Street would be very different today, since Thrift's Grocery Warehouse and the prominent clock tower were demolished in 1962.

Above: Readers may well recognise this vintage photograph of Tamworth Road, taken by David Bradley at the beginning of 1959. On the right, we can see a young schoolboy in a John Ruskin uniform, walking south from West Croydon Railway Station towards the former school premises. By the time this picture was taken the school would have moved to Shirley, so perhaps he was just on his way home after attending the new school. The trolleybus in the distance is heading for Station Road after crossing North End and then on to Crystal Palace. The No.654 travelling in the opposite direction is on route to Sutton. A classic Austin Metropolitan is parked on the roadside near to the Esso Garage. The 'Metro' was sold in the UK between April 1957 and February 1961, and could be purchased for just over £700. In May 1960, Car Mart Ltd presented Princess Margaret with a specially prepared Metropolitan finished in black with gold trim as a wedding present.

Below: This is a unique view of two trolleybuses passing on the end of Tamworth Road. The sandwich board on the elderly gentleman stood on Reeves Corner, could well say 'The End is Nigh' for trolleybuses on Route 630. When this picture was taken Route 654 had already gone and this is where the two routes had previously diverged. Subsequently, not only were the trolleybuses to disappear but also many of the buildings in Tamworth Road, although the Eagle Public House building remains much as it was then. This end of Tamworth Road used to be a comprehensive shopping area in 1959 but few shoppers are found in this location now. Parking of private cars has been banished to nearby multi-storey car parks. Today, it is pencils rather than pints at the former pub, as the building was transformed into an education and community centre.

Right: A trip down memory lane for those readers who remember this area of West Croydon. The cars are parked on the roadside on Pitlake in August, 1961. Behind them in the photograph are Handcroft Services, a BP garage and 19th century Derby Arms. Built in 1832, the pub became known as a centre for hunting enthusiasts. In those days, before motorised transport, many customers travelled by horse-drawn vehicles, and the Derby Arms provided excellent stabling facilities for their visitors. Readers may recognise the pub from the 1990s as The Paddock, or more recently G's Bar.

Above: A MkII Hillman Minx and a single-decker bus overtake the No.68 bus to South Croydon, as they travel along North End. The mainly female shoppers are dressed up for the cold in this chilly afternoon from February, 1958. On the right, just by the traffic lights at the pedestrian crossing is Horne Bros Ltd gentlemen's tailors and outfitters. The Croydon branch of Horne Bros opened in November, 1938, at 38-40 North End, in premises formerly occupied by Charles Baker, tailors and outfitters. It closed in February, 1991, and more recently will be recognised as the premises of JJB Sports. The clock on the left remains today as do many of the buildings, but this is now a traffic-free pedestrianised area with a massive tree situated in the centre of the road.

Left: It is a miserable day in the centre of Croydon as we can clearly see in this photograph. The distinctive bollards are in Church Street near the Hippodrome and the junction with Surrey Street. Very few people are around so it could be very early or perhaps a Sunday. Ogden Smith is inviting us to 'Come Inside' and view his latest range of cycles. The 'Ogden Smith Worker' is setting a new standard in value at just £4. The lone gentleman has propped his cycle up on the kerb as it looks as though he is about to deliver something, maybe a paper from the local newsagents. On another day you would be able to see a stall on the the popular six-day market on Surrey Street.

Two early morning pictures taken along George Street, outside the Railway Hotel, directly opposite East Croydon Station. The Railway Hotel opened its doors in 1841 in response to needs generated by the station, which had begun operating that same year on the London and Brighton Railway, and was a favourite watering hole for many. Readers may not even recognise this as George Street as the outlook has changed completely. The years which followed saw even more changes, with the removal of buildings on both sides of the road. The Suttons building was to be replaced by Essex House office block, which in turn was later demolished. Even the clock tower in the distance has gone. It was part of Thrift's Grocery Warehouse, which was sadly demolished by Croydon Council in 1962. Exciting new developments in the late 1990s gave Croydon the new Tramlink, with George Street forming part of the new route.

L ong hair, mini skirts, and a Mark 1 Ford Cortina indicate this photograph was taken in the mid-1960s. This busy scene looking along North End was probably taken on a Saturday with the town full of shoppers. Two-way traffic was still the norm with the No 194 bus passing Littlewoods department store on the left and Allders on the right. This was the heyday of boutiques where the younger generation congregated to shop for their short dresses with flowing sleeves, and the ankle-strap shoes and knee-length boots that had ousted the pointed toes of a few years earlier. In the 1960s men's fashions moved far more slowly than did women's, and the knee-length 'car coat' was to remain popular wear for many years. Who would have thought at this time that this expanse of road would be pedestrianised less than 25 years later?

THE WAR YEARS

purpose-built boxes to and from lessons. At the start of September 1939, any youngster being evacuated from the major urban areas clutched a battered suitcase in one hand and a gas mask in the other. For two to five year old children there was a red and blue mask known as the 'Mickey Mouse' mask even though it doesn't look anything like the cartoon

GAS EXERCISE
HAVE YOUR GAS MASK READY

In the late 1930s, as the outbreak of war seemed a certainty, civil defence groups began organising their strategies and trained members in the use of measures that would help combat the effects of modern warfare on the civilian population. The issuing of gas masks and instruction in their use was one such measure. All schoolchildren were issued with them in the early summer of 1939 and they carried them in

mouse! Because many small children were frightened of gas masks, bright colours and the friendly name were used.

Babies also had special helmets into which mothers would have to pump air with a bellows. Even the police were expected to don the less than flattering apparatus but it was a wise precaution even if the fear of a gas attack never materialised.

Above: Heartfelt and passionate embraces take place between women and their menfolk at this farewell gathering from Croydon Barracks in Mitcham Road. Those present try and keep upbeat but this is a sad moment for all concerned as the troops say their goodbyes before going off to war. No amount of prayers could guarantee a safe return for the troops so this could be the last time they would see each other. Wartime was possibly the worst time to forge relationships and marry, yet incredibly more couples than ever tied-the-knot in the first months of the war. Half-a-million weddings took place in 1940 as men were called up to join the military. A poignant and thought provoking image.

Right: When the Blitz began in earnest people were glad to see a place of shelter. Croydon folk began to appreciate the Anderson and Morrison shelters even more when attacks upon the capital began in the early autumn of 1940. Anderson shelters were issued free to all householders who earned less than £5 a week (equivalent to £280 in 2015, when adjusted for inflation). Those with a higher income were charged £7 for their shelter. They were buried 4 ft (1.2 m) deep in the soil and then covered with soil above the roof. One and a half million shelters of this type were distributed in the UK between February 1939 and the outbreak of war. During the war a further 2.1 million were installed.

Right: Just six months before the outbreak of the Second World War, huge crowds turned out to watch a procession that was over two miles long, arranged by the Civil Defence Organisation. The streets of Croydon were lined with people of all ages as the rousing procession passed by. The aim of the event was to pull in hundreds of people who were willing to volunteer to defend the country should war break out. In between the sound of the pipes and drums of the Brigade of Guards were the rallying call messages asking Croydonians to do their patriotic duty and join the war effort. On the back of this lorry are two of the massive air raid sirens to be placed outside the town hall in Katharine Street.

Below: Following the procession in May, 1939, the massive crowds had started to disperse and one of the air raid sirens had been placed in position outside the town hall. The exhibition and demonstration of war equipment is thought to have been part of the recruitment drive. To the right of the photograph a group of civilians are being shown how to use a gas mask. The Air Raid Precautions (ARP) act came into force, compelling all local authorities to set up schemes. It required wardens, first aid, emergency ambulance, gas decontamination, rescue, repair and demolition services as well as first aid posts, gas cleansing stations and casualty clearing stations. The public were keen to help as much as possible but little did they realise what horrors were to unfold only a few months down the line.

Right: Women were conscripted in December, 1941. They were given a choice of working in industry or joining one of the auxiliary services – the Auxiliary Territorial Service (ATS), the Women's Auxiliary Air Force (WAAF) or the Women's Royal Naval Service (WRNS). The ATS was formed in 1938. Initially, the only jobs available were cooks, clerks, orderlies, storewomen or drivers. But eventually there were over 100 different roles in the ATS. They became actively involved in civil defence schemes as overnight fire watchers in factories, ambulance drivers, air raid wardens, members of first

aid parties and messengers. Such women were at risk from bombing and frequently went into areas that nobody else would. This photograph could well be a group of such brave women ambulance drivers who had been billeted to Croydon during WWII. Despite the death and destruction going on around them they still managed to maintain a wonderful London humour. Even the future Queen, Princess Elizabeth drove an ambulance during her wartime service in the ATS.

Left: The war on the home front took on many forms between 1939 and 1945, and one of them was the drive to increase locally grown food production. The nation could no longer rely on imported food with German U-boats preying on merchant ships. With the men away fighting, women had to step in and fill the gaps. Hence the Women's Land army was created. The 80,000 women who joined up to the Land Army were sent wherever they were needed. The agricultural work was often hard and unfamiliar, but the girls achieved a new-found sense of independence and purpose, and lifetime friendships were forged.

The group of girls seen here are working hard a few miles away from Croydon on Hook Farm. They lived either on the farm where they worked, or in hostels. Initially, Land Girls earned £1.85 for a minimum of 50 hours work a week. In 1944, wages were increased by £1 to £2.85. Wages were paid by the farmer, rather than directly by the state.

During World War II all sorts of essential and non-essential foods were rationed, as well as clothing, furniture and petrol. Before the war started Britain imported about 55 million tons of food a year from other countries. After war was declared in September, 1939, the British government had to cut down on the amount of food it brought in from abroad and decided to introduce a system of rationing. People were encouraged to provide their own food at home. The 'Dig for Victory' campaign started in October, 1939, and called for every man and woman to keep an allotment. Lawns and flowerbeds were turned into vegetable gardens. Chickens, rabbits, goats and pigs were reared in town parks and gardens. Ration Books were issued to make sure everybody got a fair share. They contained coupons that

had to be handed to the shopkeepers every time rationed goods were bought. There was a shortage of materials to make clothes. People were also urged to 'Make do and mend' so that clothing factories and workers could be used to make items, such as parachutes and uniforms, needed in the battle against Germany. Every item of clothing was given a value in coupons.

Each person was given 66 coupons to last them a year. Children were allocated an extra 10 clothing coupons above the standard ration to allow for growing out of clothes during a year. This did not prevent children having to wear 'hand me downs' from older brothers and sisters. In a make do and mend environment, trousers and skirts were patched and darned, old jumpers were unpicked and the wool used to make new garments.

Right: All the family was roped in to help build the wartime defences around this house in Whitworth Road, South Norwood, only a few 100 yards from Selhurst Park. Tons of sand had been dumped on the road outside No.68, and the sandbagging process was well underway. The women held the sacks open while the men shovelled away. The object being to protect as much of the front window and doorway as possible, without totally blocking the light. World War Two

in Europe began only a few months earlier on 3 September, 1939, when the Prime Minister of Britain, Neville Chamberlain, declared war on Germany. For the first time, civilians were likely to be directly involved in the fighting. Shelters were being hastily built and air raid precautions taken. As work continued, neighbours joined in to lend a hand. It was part of British life that everyone who could mucked in to help whatever the circumstances. It had also become part of British culture and customs that everything stops for tea - even building wartime defences. The tea break is so famous there is even a song about it. This was not just an ordinary house however, it was to double up as a reporting station, for those wanting to do

their special bit for the war effort. The precautions were obviously worth it as the houses look almost identical today over 75 years later - a testament to the hard work of the Croydon people.

Right: Nylon stockings were a luxury item during WWII and as they were subject to rationing, quiet hard to get. They were very desirable, however, as it was very fashionable to wear them. As we can see in this photograph above, women often just drew a seam on the back of their legs to give the impression they were wearing nylons. There was a product on sale in chemists called "Leg-tan" but if you couldn't afford it, they used gravy browning powder, made in water as normal then applied to the legs and allowed to dry before the seam was drawn with eyebrow pencil by another female. It was crucial to achieve knockout legs for that important dance!

Right: A sad time for all the residents in Cranmer Road, after the bombing in July, 1944, when they returned home to find the devastation caused by the V-1 flying bombs or doodlebugs, as they were nicknamed. We became used to that awful silence when the engine cut out on the pilotless machines, and shuddered while waiting for the crash as the high explosive bomb finally found its target. During the summer of 1944 over 100 of these

bombs were launched against Britain every day. More fell on Croydon than any other London borough. It was an upsetting time for residents can be seen salvaging what few possessions they could but most were only left with memories. It was agony to live through but it did have some lighter moments and the wonderful support everyone gave each other was beyond belief.

Left: A number of the men in this photograph were part of the Air Raid Precautions team (APR). As part of their duty was being able to establish and advise on air raids, they needed to be quite sure what was flying overhead. They had taken classes in aircraft recognition as part of their training. In addition, the Home Guard was formed as a back-up to the army to defend the towns and villages of the UK should the Germans invade. Initially, they were armed with only what could be scrounged and private weapons. They eventually were properly armed and usually consisted of men in reserved occupations, those unable to fight due to a medical condition, or those who were too old to fight. This group of wardens would have plenty to see in the coming weeks as the Battle of Britain raged overhead.

Right: The battle of the skies over South East England brought its own problems on the ground. The very welcome success of the Spitfires and Hurricanes resulted in ten German planes being brought down over Orpington and Chislehurst and two more close to Biggin Hill. A German Heinkel III bomber crashed into a residential area only a few miles from Croydon, killing one person and trapping two others in the ruins. An added danger was that there were a total of 29 unexploded bombs in the wreckage. This photograph shows some of the bombs being examined by service personnel, while a rescue squad surveys the damage nearby.

Below: Life in Croydon was transformed by the Second World War. The proximity to the capital and to RAF stations at Kenley and Biggin Hill, as well as the fighter planes stationed at its airport, meant air raids over Croydon were a regular and terrifying reality. Thousands of homes were destroyed or damaged by air raids and more than 750 civilians lost their lives. The Borough of Croydon probably suffered more than any other from V1 flying-bombs, known as the "Doodlebug". It is estimated that a total of 142 landed on the Borough centre and another 19 on the fringes. A staggering 59,000 houses were damaged and of these 1,400 were completely destroyed. In this image from June, 1944, crowds of residents and onlookers had gathered to check the damage, near the scene of the latest V1 (Robotplane) strike in Elgin Road.

Right: Croydon was a leading town in the Wartime National Savings movement. Campaigns were promoted throughout the war and the National Savings shop opened at 72, George Street (where Suffolk House now stands) on 4 March, 1940. This was provided free of rent and rates. On 25 May, 1940, a salvage shop also opened on George Street and this was followed by another seven around the district. The Salvage Committee and its many voluntary workers were collecting waste metal, rags, paper and food. A

salvage exhibition was held at the badly damaged Crown Hotel in the week commencing 7 June. A salvage parade was held on 14 June, where goods were collected in even greater numbers. This picture shows the Mayor, Alderman Harding, (seated right) and the Town Clerk (seated left), making personal purchases of savings certificates during National Savings Week 1940.

Below: A damaged Messchersmitt 109 was placed on display at the Fairfield as a fundraiser for the Local Spitfire fund. The Croydon Fighter Plane Fund was opened in mid-July 1940, to raise £5000 for a plane to be called 'Croydon' and bear the Croydon Borough coat of arms. To help the fund. The Air Ministry loaned a Messerschmitt which had been shot down that summer in Surrey. It was displayed at the Fairfield car park for 10 days in late August and some 26,000 people paid to see it.

There were joyous scenes the length and breadth of the country on VJ Day, as the official end to the war was announced on 15 August, 1945. Joy and euphoria took hold as Japan surrendered to the Allies after almost six years of fighting. British Prime Minister, Clement Atlee, confirmed the news in a broadcast saying: 'The last of our enemies is laid low'. The day was greeted with equal degrees of relief and jubilation.

Several months earlier on 8 May, 1945, residents in Lansdowne Road in Purley, were celebrating on VE Day. The Second World War was over and this scene was repeated up and down the country. Trestle tables and benches were borrowed from church halls and school dining rooms. Union flags and bunting fluttered from windows and lampposts on every street. Purley celebrated in style with a street party for the whole neighbourhood. Mums spent all of the weeks rations providing sandwiches and cakes and homemade lemonade for a treat that had been denied to us for so long. There was dancing in the streets, fireworks and festivities throughout the day and into the evening.

FAMOUS CROYDONIANS
Some of the people you might not realise have links with Croydon

Croydon and the surrounding areas have entertained a multitude of famous people. A selection of those who were born in the London Borough of Croydon, or have lived within the borders of the borough are...

Dame Peggy Ashcroft, the Shakespearian actress, was born in Croydon and lived in George Street as a child. She is honoured in the naming of the Ashcroft Theatre, part of the Fairfield Halls. The Academy Award-winning, legendary actress maintained her status in the British acting elite for decades. She was made a Dame of the British Empire by Queen Elizabeth II in 1956.

David Herbert Richards Lawrence, lived at Colworth Road, Addiscombe. He was an English novelist, poet, playwright, essayist, literary critic and painter who published as D. H. Lawrence. In 1908, Lawrence qualified as a teacher and found employment at Davidson Road School in Croydon. His works are heavily autobiographical and describe the experiences of his early years. Lawrence is perhaps best known for his novels Sons and Lovers, The Rainbow, Women in Love and Lady Chatterley's Lover.

Raymond Chandler, screenwriter and author of 'The Big Sleep' and 'The Long Goodbye', has been honoured with an English Heritage blue plaque on his childhood home in Upper Norwood, Croydon. Chandler achieved worldwide acclaim for his series of novels featuring private detective Philip Marlowe and for his work on classic movies. During the 1940s several of Chandler's novels were adapted into film. His reputation was cemented when he was Oscar nominated for co-scriptwriting 'Double Indemnity' in 1943. He went on to write the original screenplay of the 1945 hit movie 'The Blue Dahlia'.

John Whitgift, John Whitgift was the Archbishop of Canterbury from 1583 to his death in 1604. He set up a charitable foundation, now The Whitgift Foundation, in Croydon, the site of a palace, a summer retreat of Archbishops of Canterbury. It supports homes for the elderly and infirm, and runs three independent schools – Whitgift School, a prestigious institute of learning founded in 1596, Trinity School of John Whitgift and, more recently, Old Palace School for girls, which is housed in the former Croydon Palace. He died in 1604 and was buried in Croydon at the Parish Church of St John Baptist (now Croydon Minster).

Whitgift Street near Lambeth Palace (the official London residence of the Archbishop of Canterbury) is named after him. The Whitgift Centre, a major shopping centre in Croydon, is also named after him.

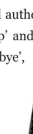

Sir David Lean, film director, was born in Croydon on 25 March, 1908. An important British film maker, David Lean was brought up in a strict Quaker family (ironically, as a child, he wasn't allowed to go to the movies). During the 1920s he briefly considered the possibility of becoming an accountant like his father before finding a job at Gaumont British Studios in 1927. He was taken on as a teaboy, promoted to clapperboy, and soon rose to the position of third assistant director. By 1930 he was working as an editor on newsreels. Best remembered for big-screen epics such as The Bridge on the River Kwai (1957), Lawrence of Arabia (1962), and Doctor Zhivago (1965); for perhaps the most highly regarded of all the adaptations of Dickens' novels with Great Expectations (1946) and Oliver Twist (1948).

Sir Arthur Conan Doyle, was born on 22 May, 1859, in Edinburgh and is one of the truly great authors in our history. Doyle's house still stands in Croydon and is a sight to see for any avid Sherlock Holmes fans. Conan Doyle lived at Tennison Road, South Norwood, from 1891 to 1894, but, contrary to popular belief, did not use the area as the setting for the Sherlock Holmes story The Adventure of the Norwood Builder. This story, for the most part, takes place in Lower Norwood (today known as West Norwood). In 1891, Conan Doyle moved to the South Norwood with his first wife Louise and their two-year-old daughter. His son Kingsley was born there on November 15, 1892.

Peter Wilton Cushing was born on 26 May, 1913, in Kenley, to Nellie Maria (King) and George Edward Cushing, a quantity surveyor. He and his older brother, David, were raised first in Dulwich Village and then later back in Surrey. In 1926, his father built Clearview, an Art Deco house on St James Road, Purley. It was here that Cushing remained until early adulthood. From an early age, Cushing was attracted to acting. He is mainly known for his prolific appearances in Hammer films, in which he played strong character roles like the sinister scientist Baron Frankenstein, Sherlock Holmes and the vampire hunter Dr. Van Helsing, among many other roles.

Miles Malleson was born in Croydon. He was an actor and dramatist, particularly remembered for his appearances in British comedy films of the 1930s to 1960s. Actor, playwright and screenwriter, Malleson's list of credits reads like a history of British cinema in the first half of the 20th century. Over 30 years he appeared in nearly 100 films, featuring in everything from Alfred Hitchcock thrillers and Ealing comedies to Hammer horrors.

Charles Burgess Fry, Sportsman, born in Croydon and academically brilliant he represented England at cricket and football, he was also a great athlete.

Consider David Beckham, combined with Kevin Pietersen, and yet with the ability to set a world record for the long jump. Fry was all of that and more. He was so famous, Albania asked him to be their king - he declined. And yes, Stephen Fry is a descendant of the great man.

Jacqueline du Pré, British cellist, acknowledged as one of the greatest players of the instrument, but whose career was cut short by Multiple Sclerosis, which forced her to stop performing at the age of 28, and led to her premature death. She lived in Purley and attended Croydon High School, an independent day school for girls in South Croydon. From an early age, du Pré was entering and winning local music competitions alongside her sister, flautist Hilary du Pré. In

1965, at the age of 20, du Pré recorded the Elgar Concerto in E Minor with the London Symphony Orchestra and Sir John Barbirolli, which brought her international recognition. Du Pré died in London on 19th October, 1987, at 42.

Frederick Betts, donated Betts Park and built large areas in Croydon and Penge. Frederick Betts was born in Croydon in 1859. Frederick, a builder and major property owner, was a well-known local figure. He donated £3,000 to Penge Council to fund the purchase of Betts Park in memory of his mother Sarah in 1927. Oak Lawn, at one time the vicarage of Holy Trinity, Penge, on the corner of Croydon Road and Anerley Road, was purchased with the money. He died in 1944.

Samuel Coleridge-Taylor (1875–1912), composer; Born and died in Croydon, incorporated African-American folk music into his compositions. Coleridge-Taylor (below) was brought up in Croydon by Alice Hare Martin and her father Benjamin Holmans, and lived at 30 Dagnall Park, Selhurst. Coleridge-Taylor's greatest work was undoubtedly his cantata "Hiawatha's Wedding Feast," which was widely performed by choral groups in England during his lifetime and in the decades after his death. There are two blue plaques in his memory, one in Dagnall Park and the other in St Leonards Road, Croydon, the house in which he died. A metal figure in the likeness of Coleridge-Taylor has been installed in Charles Street, Croydon.

Cicely Mary Barker, illustrator and artist, created the famous Flower Fairies books was born 28 June, 1895, at 66,Waddon Road, Croydon. In 1908, at 13 years of age, she entered an evening class at the Croydon School of Art, and attended the school into the 1940s. Her earliest professional work included greeting cards and juvenile magazine illustrations, and her first book, Flower Fairies of the Spring, was published in 1923. Barker died in 1973.

Frederick George Creed, electrical engineer and inventor of the teleprinter; lived at 20, Outram Road, Addiscombe. Creed's home in East Croydon, is marked with a commemorative English Heritage blue plaque. He moved to Croydon from Glasgow in 1909 along with six of his mechanics, in order to be closer to the Post Office headquarters in London. Creed died at home in 1957 at the age of 86.

Alfred Russel Wallace was a British naturalist, explorer, geographer, anthropologist, and biologist. He independently proposed a theory of evolution by natural selection and prompted Charles Darwin to reveal his own unpublished theory sooner than he had intended. He was considered the 19th century's leading expert on the geographical distribution of animal species and is sometimes called the "father of biogeography". There is an English Heritage blue plaque on a house which Wallace called "Pen-y-Bryn" (top of the hill and subsequently numbered 44) in St Peter's Road, Croydon, where he lived in the early 1880s.

R.F. Delderfield, was a popular writer and dramatist who lived at 22 Ashburton Avenue, Addiscombe, from 1918-1923. His "Avenue" series is based on his life in Addiscombe & Shirley Park. Many of his works have been adapted for television and are still widely read. Several of Delderfield's historical novels and series involve young men who return from war and lead lives in England that allow the author to portray the sweep of English history and delve deeply into social history from the Edwardian era to the early 1960s.

British actor **Edward Woodward** made a highly successful transition into Hollywood stardom in the mid 1980s thanks to a popular TV series, The Equalizer, earning him the 1986 Golden Globe Award for Best Television Drama Actor. He was born in June 1930, in Croydon and received his early education at various schools before becoming a student at Kingston College. He was reputedly torn between becoming an actor or a professional footballer. Woodward was on the books of Leyton Orient and Brentford, making three appearances in the Football League for the latter. His professional acting debut was at the Castle Theatre, Farnham, in 1946.

Purley born actor **Richard Stanley Thorpe**, was born in 1932. His first job was at his father's shoe-making factory but he was keen to be an actor and joined the local amateur dramatics society before studying at the Guildhall School of Music and Drama.

His breakthrough part was that of Squadron Leader Henry Maudslay in the 1955 film The Dam Busters, but became better known to millions of television viewers as Alan Turner, the landlord of The Woolpack in the Yorkshire-based soap Emmerdale. A pillar of the show, he became Emmerdale's longest-running cast member. He died in 2013, at the age of 81.

And they're not the only ones...

Other famous faces who have lived in or were born in Croydon include, Topshop boss **Sir Philip Green**, model **Kate Moss**, comic actor **Will Hay**, artist **Tracey Emin**, illusionist **Derren Brown**, footballer, **Ian Wright**, England football manager **Roy Hodgson**, entertainer **Roy Hudd**, actors **Deryck Guyler** and **Martin Clunes** and actress **June Brown** from Eastenders.

It's quite a mixed group but it goes to show how Croydon's influence has extended into many different fields.

Born in 1930 in Edinburgh, popular entertainer **Ronnie Corbett** lived in Shirley for many years until his death in 2016. He was affectionately known as a 'national treasure' with a career spanning more than 60 years. During this time he was one of the most familiar faces on British television screens, largely part through his decades-long double act with Ronnie Barker. A partnership that began on "The Frost Report" in the 1960s led to the pair's BBC show "The Two Ronnies", which featured a number of memorable comedy moments - including the hilarious "Fork Handles" sketch, which attracted a TV audience of 17million. He was a keen golfer and appeared in many celebrity and pro-am charity events. A keen cricket and football fan, he supported his local football club, Crystal Palace, as well as his home town club Hearts. Ronnie Corbett was famously only 5ft 1in, but he was a giant of comedy and never short of a funny line or gesture. In this photograph from April, 1973, we can see Ronnie jokingly standing on the tee box to gain a few extra inches. He was making his bow as the newly appointed Captain of the Variety Club of Great Britain Golfing Society in a charity match at Addington Golf Club.

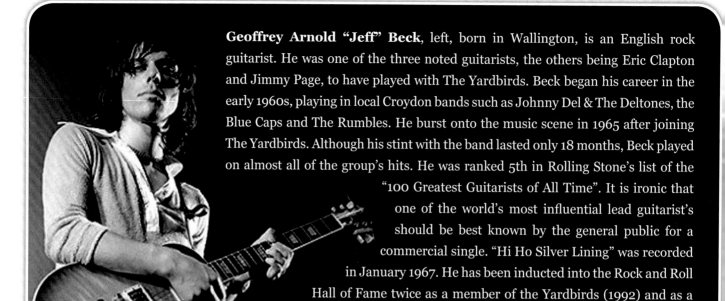

Geoffrey Arnold "Jeff" Beck, left, born in Wallington, is an English rock guitarist. He was one of the three noted guitarists, the others being Eric Clapton and Jimmy Page, to have played with The Yardbirds. Beck began his career in the early 1960s, playing in local Croydon bands such as Johnny Del & The Deltones, the Blue Caps and The Rumbles. He burst onto the music scene in 1965 after joining The Yardbirds. Although his stint with the band lasted only 18 months, Beck played on almost all of the group's hits. He was ranked 5th in Rolling Stone's list of the "100 Greatest Guitarists of All Time". It is ironic that one of the world's most influential lead guitarist's should be best known by the general public for a commercial single. "Hi Ho Silver Lining" was recorded in January 1967. He has been inducted into the Rock and Roll Hall of Fame twice as a member of the Yardbirds (1992) and as a solo artist (2009).

In Music

Ralph McTell, brought up in Croydon, is a singer-songwriter and acoustic guitar player who has been an influential figure on the UK folk music scene since the 1960s. He attended the John Ruskin Grammar School. McTell is best known for his song "Streets of London", which has been covered by over 200 artists around the world, and for his tale of Irish emigration, "From Clare to Here". "Streets of London" was released as a single in December, 1974. It rocketed up the charts to No. 2 over the Christmas period, became a worldwide million-seller and won McTell the Ivor Novello Award.

Peter Sarstedt is an Northern Indian-born British singer-songwriter and multi-instrumentalist. His family moved to England in 1954 with him going to the Heath Clark School in Croydon. Sarstedt is perhaps most famously known for his song Where Do You go To, My Lovely which topped the charts in 1969. In the same year he was joint winner of the prestigious Ivor Novello songwriting award, sharing his prize with David Bowie's Space Oddity. He was once reported to have said "I prefer Croydon to anywhere else because I understand it. I know its vibe and I don't feel a stranger with the people here."

Raymond Ian Burns known by the stage name Captain Sensible, is a singer, songwriter and guitarist. He was born in Balham, in 1954 and later went to Stanley Technical School for Boys in South Norwood. Sensible co-founded the punk rock band The Damned. He embarked on a solo career during the 1980s, following a UK number one hit with his cover of "Happy Talk". His signature headwear is a red beret.

Kirsty MacColl, English singer and songwriter, (right) was the daughter of folk singer Ewan MacColl and dancer Jean Newlove. She and her brother, Hamish MacColl, grew up with their mother in Croydon, where Kirsty attended Park Hill Primary School, Monks Hill High School and John Newnham High School. She recorded several pop hits between the early 1980s and the 1990s, including "There's a Guy Works Down the Chip Shop Swears He's Elvis" and cover versions of Billy Bragg's "A New England". In addition, she sang on hit recordings produced by her husband Steve Lillywhite, most notably "Fairytale of New York" by The Pogues. Sadly she died at the age of 41, after being hit by a boat in Mexico.

The list goes on.....

Desmond Dekker, ska musician, lived in Thornton Heath, Status Quo frontman **Francis Rossi**, **Matthew Charles Fisher** (born in Addiscombe, musician, songwriter and producer. He is best known for playing the Hammond organ on the 1967 single, "A Whiter Shade of Pale" by Procol Harum,

A selection of the famous alumni from the BRIT School for Performing Arts and Technology include **Adele, Jessie J, the Feeling, Amy Winehouse, Kate Nash, Katie Melua, the Kooks, Leona Lewis,** all singers, songwriters and musicians who spent time in Croydon.

Croydon once hosted some of the biggest names in music on the planet.

It's not just the underground music scene that has thrived in Croydon. Back in its heyday, old Croydon music venue, The Greyhound saw the likes of **Jimi Hendrix, The Who, David Bowie** and **Queen** performing. And that's not all, the world's most famous band; **The Beatles** appeared in Croydon on three occasions in 1963. Initially, in March, at the ABC and on the following two performances at none other than our very own Fairfield Halls!

In fiction

Sarah Jane Smith, (right), played by Elisabeth Sladen, was the popular fictional companion of the third and fourth doctors in the television series "Doctor Who." The Doctor claims to have returned Sarah to her home which is Hill View Road in South Croydon. However, as the TARDIS departs, Sarah realises that she isn't on Hill View Road or anywhere near it. Thirty years later in the tenth doctor adventure, "School Reunion," we would learn that she is correct. She is, in fact, in Aberdeen. K9 Mark III was delivered to Sarah Jane's aunt Lavinia's South Croydon home, in 1978. Sarah Jane had already moved out of the house by that time and was travelling extensively.

Jeremy "Jez" Osbourne and **Mark Corrigan**, the fictional protagonists from the Channel 4 sitcom Peep Show, live in a flat in West Croydon.

The fictional character of Captain **Kevin Darling** was played by **Tim McInnerry** who lived in Croydon in the BBC sitcom "Blackadder Goes Forth" lived in Croydon with his girlfriend Doris. Darling was also a wicket keeper for the Croydon Gentlemen cricket team.

The popular BBC sitcom "Terry and June," starring **Terry Scott** and **June Whitfield**, was set in Purley.

ON THE MOVE IN CROYDON

The R33 class of British rigid airships were built for the Royal Naval Air Service during the First World War, but were not completed until after the end of hostilities by which time the RNAS had become part of the Royal Air Force. The lead ship, R33, went on to serve successfully for 10 years.

R33 first flew on 6 March 1919, and was sent to RAF Pulham in Norfolk. Between then and October 14, R33 made 23 flights totalling 337 hours flying time. One of these, a flight promoting 'Victory Bonds' even included a brass band playing in the top machine gun post. In 1920 she was demilitarised and given over to civilian work. After an overhaul, R33 was based at Croydon Airport, moored to a portable mast. In June, 1921, it was used by the Metropolitan Police to observe traffic at the Epsom Derby, and in July appeared in the Hendon Air Pageant before flying to Cardington, Bedfordshire, where she was laid up for three years.

During this time, further tasks were still being allocated to the ship, for example after dark flights over South London and Surrey to view from the air the new airport lighting system at Croydon Airport. The ship was also involved in helping with traffic control by assisting with the police during the Epsom and Ascot race weeks. To avoid the ship having to return to Pulham, it was moored to a wooden mast at Croydon Airport on the nights of 14 and 15 July, 1921.

Right: This is a great Edwardian era view of East Croydon and New Croydon stations. The nostalgic scene was photographed a few years after the two stations merged into a single station, with three island platforms. Following the merger in 1897-98, they kept separate booking accounts until the formation of the Southern Railway. The Croydon station originally began passenger services on 12 July, 1941, run by London & Brighton Railway

(L&BR). A number of hotels and hostelries sprang up around this time and The Railway Hotel, opposite the station, was one of these that is well known to the people of Croydon. With the completion of the line to Victoria between 1860 and 1862, extra platforms were needed that adjoined East Croydon but ran as a separate station named New Croydon. From the opening of the stations to the 1920s, the population of Croydon increased massively and as a result the station was enlarged and rebuilt on a number of occasions. Today, East Croydon is one of the busiest non-terminal stations in London and it is also one of the busiest non-terminal through stations in the UK.

Left: Before 1860 practically all road transport was horse-drawn and powered machines to ride upon were unknown. At the end of the 19th century, road transport was still almost entirely dependant on the horse, which meant that it was slow and only suitable for short distance travel. Light horse-drawn cabs, which could be manoeuvred down London's maze of streets, were fashionable among rich Londoners. We can see the sign for Central Croydon railway station, which is off to the right on this old photograph. It was deemed a largely unsuccessful venture by the London Brighton and South Coast Railway, to bring trains closer to the centre of Croydon, as East Croydon station was deemed too far from the busy town centre. It originally opened in 1868 and closed in 1871. It then reopened in 1886, before closing permanently in 1890. Subsequently the site was used for the building of Croydon Town Hall in 1892–1896.

Below: This is a typical street scene from Croydon at the start of the 20th century. We can see from the clock that it is just after midday as the No.38 tram makes its way up the High Street passing the old Post Office building on the left, and the junction with Park Street on the right, as we look at it. In the distance we can see the almshouses and the Allders departmental store. The destination board of the tram shows a route running between Thornton Heath and Purley, which remained until the Croydon system was joined to the LCC network at Norbury. With through running of the LCC routes 16/18 from 1926 onwards,

this local route was curtailed initially at the former Davis Theatre, but later extended a few hundred yards to Coombe Road to ease road congestion outside the theatre. Once a very busy thoroughfare, traffic management schemes of the late 1990s take all but very local traffic away from this area. The clock is still in place today, outside the building that was until recently the home of Yates's Wine Lodge.

Right: Croydon Corporation Tramways No.39 trundles along George Street, on the Addiscombe branch line. This service was discontinued in 1927. The first electric trams appeared on London's streets in 1901. However, by the 1930s trams were seen as noisy and dangerous to other road users. In 1931 a commission of inquiry recommended trams be replaced by trolleybuses, but many trams were temporarily reprieved by the outbreak of the Second World War. On the right, is the famous Allders

store and in the distance under the Bovril sign is an early Saxone shoe shop. Allders flagship Croydon store, which opened in 1862, was the fourth largest department store in Britain and boasted the largest carpet department in Europe. The now defunct Saxone footwear company was formed in 1908, in Kilmarnock. After a gap of over 70 years trams now once again run down this street to Addiscombe.

This is a great picture, particulary if you are a lover of vintage cars, with a number of them parked outside the booking office at East Croydon Station. On 12 July, 1841 the London & Brighton Railway (L&BR) began passenger services through Croydon station (now East Croydon) on the Brighton Line from London Bridge to Haywards Heath. The station was designed by the architect David Mocatta, the second station in the town since the London and Croydon Railway (L&CR) had opened its Croydon station (now West Croydon) in June 1839. In 1846 The L&BR and the L&CR amalgamated to form the London, Brighton and South Coast Railway, and the two stations were shortly renamed East Croydon and West Croydon to avoid confusion. On the left we can see T. Walton (London) Ltd, fruiterers. Founded by Lambeth-born Thomas Walton, this company was incorporated in the early 1920s. They appear to have specialised in railway station fruitery, as 25 of these branches were in stations including both busy central stations such as King's Cross and London Bridge, as well as this one in Croydon.

These two pictures span 25 years but in each case they were taken shortly before the system was closed - the trams in 1935 and the trolleybuses in 1959. Little seems to have changed over that period except, perhaps, for the provision of a roundabout to enable the trolleybuses to turn. However it could be said that only the trams actually went to Crystal Palace whereas the trolleybuses, for most of their life, never did. Dominating the area is the Crystal Palace Park, with its museum on Anerley Hill recording the area's rich heritage from the rein of Queen Victoria, when the Crystal Palace was moved here from Hyde Park and remained until 1936, when it was tragically destroyed by fire. The park was an ambitious project designed to display Victorian grandeur and innovation. It was financed by visitors who paid at a turnstile to enter the park and is one of the largest parks in South London. A ride down Anerley Hill on an open deck tram car must have been an experience in itself although the comfort of a trolleybus in inclement weather was probably to be preferred. Both tram No.345 and trolleybus No.89 were scrapped within a month of services ceasing.

Above: Not everyone can remember the clanking noise of the trams as they trundled through the streets of West Croydon. This view along London Road, towards North End in the late 1940s, gives some indication of what it was like. The photograph was taken from outside The Old Fox & Hounds, looking towards the traffic lights and the junction with Station Road. Trams and cars took up the same piece of road and it's a wonder that there weren't more accidents. The driver of this old Hillman 14 or Austin 16, has decided to go for it and pass the stationary traffic on his left. The London Transport tram, type, E3, is on route No.42 between Thornton Heath Pond and The Greyhound.

Right: This busy scene at the junction of London Road/North End and Station Road is similar to the image on the back page of this Croydon - The Golden Years publication. Both photographs were taken by David Bradley from a first floor bedroom at The Railway Bell Hotel, on the south west corner of the easily recognisable junction. This location is unique for in the 1940s it was the only place in London where all forms of surface transport could have been photographed - trams, trolleybuses, Central and County buses, Green Line coaches, steam freight and electric suburban trains. Until its conversion to 'The Arkright's Wheel', it was 'The Railway Bell Hotel', the stone bell of which can still be seen above, along with the inscription. The No.654 Sutton trolleybus is turning out of Station Road, in front of the Woodhouse & Son store at the end of the 1950s, as Saturday shoppers wait to cross the road.

Above: It was a very proud day for the 32nd Surrey Battalion Home Guard as they take part in the parade along Katharine Street during World War II. Crowds had come out in force to cheer them on as they pass by in formation, on their BSA motorcycles. The BSA M20 was a British motorcycle made by Birmingham Small Arms Company (BSA) at their factory in Small Heath, Birmingham. Although initially viewed as a near failure by the War Office in 1936, the M20 evolved into one of the longest-serving motorcycles in the history of British military motorcycling. The Home Guard had to defend its home patch by whatever means were available and to act as the eyes of the Regular Army.

Below: Croydon Airport returned to civil control in February 1946. Following the end of the war it was realised that post war airliners and cargo aircraft would be larger and air traffic would intensify. The urban spread of south London and the surrounding villages growing into towns, had enclosed Croydon Airport and left it no room for expansion. Heathrow was therefore designated as London's airport. In the 1950s Croydon Airport was popular with flying clubs and as a base for local companies. In this photograph we can see an impressive line-up of planes and vehicles on the tarmac in front of the terminal building.

It was decided in 1952 that the airport would eventually be closed, as Blackbushe Airport in Hampshire and Northolt Aerodrome in Middlesex could accommodate European flights. This resulted in the final scheduled flight from Croydon departing on 30 September, 1959.

This is a fascinating photograph with lots to focus on, taken by David Bradley, from the bridge over the A213 Selhurst Road, in 1959. The two No.654 trolleybuses are passing each other outside Selhurst Station. On the right, just behind the trolleybus is a Routemaster double-decker No.75. London Bus Route 75 and 157 both run the length of Selhurst Road, terminating at Croydon & Lewisham. Interestingly the two cars in the foreground could both be the same make. The car on the left could be a brand new version of the older model Ford Popular, slightly ahead on the road. On the right we can also see the entrance to the Selhurst Traction & Rolling Stock maintenance depot which occupies a triangle of

and bordered on one side by the Victoria Lines and on the other by the London Bridge Lines. It was built on the site of the former Croydon Common Athletic Ground, where Crystal Palace F.C. played Football League matches between 1920 and 1924. Ahead to the left is the turning for Prince Road, which is only a short distance from Selhurst Park Stadium. Further along on the right is Heavers Meadow, an open space covering an area of 8.75 acres with a footpath through the flood meadow. Next to the advertising hoarding for Persil is a pointer to the Selhurst Arms, which used to be a popular spot for Crystal Palace football supporters on match days.

This is a classic Croydon photograph from the collection of David Bradley, which is a perfect shot of life in the late 1950s. It is taken from the Mitcham Road junction on the Lombard roundabout. Off to the right is Purley Way and the parade of shops is in Purley Way Cresent, which still looks the same today. The trolleybus, Lambretta scooter and the Ford Thames and Ford Consul at the back help us to date this image. Even the simple suit and tie, worn by the man with the child peeping out of the luxury Silver Cross pram, is further indication of the era in which this photograph was produced. The only thing that is out of place is the Morris Eight on the front left of the picture, which was manufactured in the previous decade. Today, the photographer would be standing outside the modern Lombard House office block and you would certainly not see a randomly parked scooter on a busy roundabout.

This virtually unrecognisable scene shows traffic queuing along Park Lane in 1956. The front two London Transport type 2RT:AEC Regent III buses are waiting in a line of traffic at the junction, before turning left to go out on route to Shirley and Bromley North Station, respectively. They were slightly different to other buses as they had a roofbox with a route number in it and also a green and cream livery as well as the traditional red. The mobility of the buses meant they were ideal for national advertising brands. In this image we can clearly make out advertising for brands still on sale today; Heinz soup, Black & White Whisky and Biro pens. Today, the buildings on the right would be replaced by St George's House, the former headquarters of food and consumer giants Nestle. On the opposite side would be Croydon Technical College and in between them is the new Croydon underpass.

Above: Standing out like a bright beacon, a Ford Zephyr waits in the queue of vehicles at the George Street traffic lights. It was the late 1950s with more and more new cars appearing on our streets as average living standards began to rise. Harold Macmillan became Prime Minister in 1957 and a mood of confidence filled the air. Housewives and young women began to shop at Glazer's for the latest fashions rather than running something up from a pattern out of 'Woman's Realm'. We could now pay on the 'never-never'. Hire purchase became commonplace, with so much down and then a few bob a week. Modern new developments were being built and coffee bars were replacing tea shops for the teenagers of London. This elevated view of George Street highligted very well, the balance between old and new.

Right: This photograph looking along Brighton Road is a typical street scene from the early 1960s. With no white lines, zigzags or pedestrian crossings to contend with, cars and vans could park wherever they wanted on the roadside. The Vauxhall Viva HA in the foreground would probably be one of the first produced in 1963. It proved to be a successful return by Vauxhall to the small car market and during the first 10 months, over 100,000 HA Vivas were produced. On the left we can see a lady with shopping bag, getting into one of the most recognisable models ever produced - the Mark 2 Jaguar. It was one of the iconic cars of the 1960s beloved by crooks and cops alike, and more recently was also the car used by the late John Thaw in classic TV show 'Inspector Morse'. On the right at the junction with Sanderstead Road we can see the historic watering hole the Red Deer. This local boozer dates back to the 1800s and sadly is the latest in a long line of public houses to be turned into a convenience store.

86

Right: This was a common sight on the streets of Croydon in the 1950s. Many working class people rode to work on bicycles in their regular work clothes without helmets or protective clothing. Some would have a waterproof cape in case it rained. The only really essential piece of kit were trouser clips. Car ownership was becoming more affordable for the average family but still the majority of workers used public transport, bike, or Shanks's Pony. Once at work, no one locked their bikes - they were just parked in racks with a corrugated roof to protect them from the elements. Things changed, however, when people began to vote with their wallets and their feet and swapped two wheels for four.

AROUND THE TOWN

Many bargains were to be had at Times Furnishing and other stores nearby due to the imminent widening of Crown Hill in 1930. Those shops that were affected had to save what they could from the enforced closures, and Times Furnishing were having a 'Great Re-building Sale' to get rid of as much stock as possible. The steady increase in traffic meant that some widening had to take place around Crown Hill. The 1930s economy was marked by the effects of the great depression, leading to higher unemployment and widespread poverty. However, although the downturn in the economy caused significant levels of poverty and hardship, especially in industrial heartlands around London some parts of the economy thrived. The suburbs enjoyed a building boom, helped by cheap interest rates. The family on the left, are typical of the time. He strides ahead in his natty three piece suit and hat and the lady also looks very smart in her jacket and below the knee skirt and cloche hat. The boy looks as though he is in his obligatory school uniform. Boys wore short trousers until the age of about 11 this was traditional for boys up until about 1970.

A fine array of handbags is on view, carried by the ladies in this photograph along Church Street in the late 1940s. Peacetime rationing was still in place and Britain was still battling against shortages. Inside the bags, these women probably had coupons for fresh meat, sugar and confectionery items, which continued to be rationed until the early 1950s. Clothing rationing ended in May, 1949, and C.Hewitt and Son outfitters would have seen a significant increase in trade, as Britain came out of the 'make do and mend' mentality. Many shops were long standing family businesses and Hewitt's was no exception, moving to Church Street in 1866. It has a history rooted in the community and is one of the longest running retailers of Scout Uniform dating back to 1908. The driver of the Carter Paterson van is probably making a delivery as the London based road haulage company was operating a fleet of over 1,000 vehicles by 1944. The Oxo logo on the side of the van is still instantly recognisable, promoting Oxo for 'cooking and drinking'. In later years, the humble stock cube inspired a series of TV adverts, that would be a forerunner to the soap operas of today. Viewers watched Katie produce marvellous meals for the family, with the slogan 'Oxo gives a meal man appeal!'.

Above: The Croydon store was the 12th Woolworths store to open in the UK and the 4th London store. It was opened by Frank Woolworth himself on 4 May 1912 on North End, right at the heart of the town. He had visited and shortlisted Croydon earlier, noting that the South East London location was 'fine, progressive and bustling'. The store shared its premises with the local cinema, Pyke's Cinematograph, which was a popular destination for Edwardian Croydon residents. Woolworths made the most of the opportunity, opening late to line up with films on the silver screen and offering popcorn, ice cream and many magazines and sheets of music associated with the movies. The original building was repeatedly extended and adapted to suit changing trading conditions. 1n 1929, Woolworths tooks over the cinema building next door and extended it to make a larger store. The Woolworth store served Croydon as one of the most popular stores throughout the 20th century, finally closing its doors at the end of 2008 when the chain folded in the credit crunch. Croydon features extensively in the Woolworths Museum, thanks in part to the professionalism and dedication of staff in the Local Studies Unit of Croydon Central Library.

Right: We can see from the Croydon clock tower that it is exactly 12.30pm when this rare photograph of The Croydon was taken. On the corner of High Street and Katharine Street, this was a very popular drinking establishment back in the 1960s, with many readers able to recall having a drink or two in Batty's Bar. Built at the turn of the 20th century, the Croydon became an institution in the town centre, until the mid 1990s when it became the Rat and Parrott. This fabulous building

was replaced by a less than iconic square block structure. Hockley Furrier and Express Dairy Co were had shops next to the hotel. For many women in post war Britain a fur coat represented the height of luxury, glamour and success; however it had now begun to acquire unfashionable connotations. As a result, 'fun fur' came into vogue and became a natural-looking alternative. Express Dairies was founded by George Barham in 1864 as the Express County Milk Supply Company, named after the fact that they only used express trains to get their milk to London. A sign in the shop window reminds us that more than just dairy produce was sold here – their Cornish pasties were selling for 2/8d each!

Right: Women on a mission! Get in the way of these shoppers if you dare. These ladies had queued for hours to get the best bargains on offer and can be seen here milling around in Allders traditional post Christmas January Sale. The shopping frenzy reached fever pitch at times as thrifty Croydonians snapped up bargains from the Christmas leftovers. One story tells of two women, one of them wearing a tartan hat. She took it off and placed it on the counter while she tried on another hat. The woman next to her picked up the tartan hat and tried it on,

only for the first woman to snatch it off her head and tuck it under her arm and move away without a second glance. Established by Joshua Allder in 1862, Allders developed into a chain of department stores across England and Wales. Its flagship store in Croydon was the third-largest department store in the United Kingdom.

Left: Before it was fully pedestrianised, Croydon's North End went through an intermediate period in which it was closed to private motor traffic, but still open to buses, taxis and cycles. Here we see a London Country double decker on Route 409 on its way to Godstone. Allders was founded in 1862 by Joshua Allder in Croydon the company remained with the family until the 1920s when it came under the ownership of United Drapery Stores, which decided to retain the name. UDS enjoyed huge post war success but in the 70s the recession saw the company's fortunes dwindle. North End was the home of the last Allders left standing after the company went into liquidation, which led to the collapse of the group and the closure of the Croydon store. This Allders was the fourth largest department store in Britain and boasted the largest carpet department in Europe. This image is owned by Dr Neil Clifton and used under the Creative Commons license.

One of the biggest stores in the centre of Croydon was Grant Bros department store, competing with the likes of Allders and Kennard Bros for your attention. In these two images we can see the amazing expanse of the Grant's frontage, overlooking High Street. Originally built in 1894 by Metcalfe and Jones, it was unlike the modern stores of today, with a red and grey brick exterior, styled throughout with wood panelling and wood flooring. It is also thought to be the first store in the UK to have its own generator supplied electricity. The Royal Family were also frequent visitors to Grants and on occasion the Queen would also come to the store. Times were harder after the Second World War and growing competition forced the store to close in 1985. After years of decay, the old Grade II listed Grant's building was opened as a new complex including bars, a multi-screen cinema and a health club. The High Street, once bustling with traffic, is now a tree-lined restricted traffic zone.

Right: In this photograph, possibly from the mid-1940s, just after the end of the Second World War, things are just starting to get back to some sort of normality after six years of suffering and hardship. The North End street was still empty of cars but local Croydon residents were starting resume their regular daily routines. Shoppers in this late morning scene could take a more relaxed view when shopping for clothing or quality food in the main Marks and Spencer store. Next door is George Fletcher's tailors shop and to the right of that is Durbin and McBrydes chemists, which older readers may remember for sales of cameras and film and their developing and printing service. Today, Marks & Spencer has extended the building to

take up the premises on the left at the junction with Poplar Walk. Obviously the tramlines have long gone, and North End is now a pedestrianised area with a line of small trees and seats down the centre of the road.

Left: A nice sunny day and not a car in sight, as shoppers make their way along North End. The lone means of transportation is the very basic trike used by the window cleaner, who appears to be outside on the balcony above Courlanders's Premier Jewellers. Courlanders is an independent family run business, with origins in Gracechurch Street, London, way back in 1881. The names of these shops will evoke many memories for readers, with high street names such as Boots and Freeman Hardy Willis in view, along with Edmonds Wools which was interestingly for the 1940s, buying directly from the mills. Today, these fine buildings have gone to be replaced by shops on the edge of the Whitgift Shopping Centre, officially opened in 1970.

This is an iconic view of Surrey Street Market and we make no apologies for publishing it again in this new book. There was a brisk trade on the market when this photograph was taken c1935. Although much of the old market place triangle was built up by the 19th century, a small open space remained in Market Street (immediately behind the Butter Market building) and this was the main focus of street trading. However, in 1893 the entire triangle (by this date known as Middle Row) was comprehensively cleared and redeveloped by Croydon Corporation. This event pushed all street trading activities into Surrey Street. In 1922, the street market was taken over by Croydon Corporation and re-launched as a six-day market (Monday to Saturday).

Surrey Street Market has always had a character of its very own. Many local housewives, who love a bargain as much as anyone else, have made a beeline for this spot for many years. As a kind of religious pilgrimage, Croydonians would week after week, catch a bus into town and tour the market to find the best fruit and vegetables on offer. Prices charged by market and street traders have traditionally been a few pence cheaper than on the high street and the best way to make the housekeeping stretch a bit further. This image, which is of mainly female shoppers, was taken in the 1960s.

WORK AND INDUSTRY

Right: There is a distinctly French feel to this roadworks scene on North End in 1926. The board is promoting 'Ciment Fondu', the method of making cement from limestone and low-silica bauxite, which was patented in France in 1908 by Bied of the Pavin de Lafarge Company. It is unlikely however that the workmen digging the road up outside Wilson's Tea Rooms are French.

There seems to be a large number of them all wearing traditional working clothes of a white shirt, waistcoat and flat cap. In the 19th and early 20th centuries flat caps were commonly worn throughout Britain and were even worn by fashionable young men in the 1920s. This was the year of the general strike that lasted 9 days, from 4 May to 13 May, 1926 and this predominantly male gathering may have some connection to the events surrounding the strike.

Left: As the First World War progressed and more and more men were required to maintain the British army in the field, on the 'Home Front' a manpower crisis loomed. This problem was largely tackled by mobilising women to replace the men who had gone to fight. Although women had worked in some industries for many years, the war brought women into the workplace on a scale never before witnessed. After the introduction of military conscription in March 1916, it became vital to mobilise women to fill the gaps in the factories, fields, transport and other essential areas. Women worked as conductresses (and occasionally drivers) on buses and trams, as we can see in this Croydon photograph from 1916. Between 1914 and 1918, an estimated two million women took on jobs which had been previously been filled by men. The war undoubtedly led to the social advancement of women and also to the vote being granted to women in the UK in 1918.

This is a fabulous reminder of shopping from a bygone era. It's a view of the very elegant and stylish Ladies' Department at Allders in the 1930s. The ideal Thirties woman was tall and slender with a very small waist and narrow hips, so shoulders were exaggerated with shoulder pads, white full collars and puff sleeves was designed to make waists and hips appear smaller in comparison. Staff members were also dressed smartly and were taught to be on hand to assist customers, but not too aggressively.

Above: House of Reeves in 2016, now back to 13,000 square feet of shop floor. Throughout its life the business has been a Croydon ico

House of Reeves
Landmark firm's long and proud history

IT is one of the country's leading furniture retailers with a reputation for quality that stretches way beyond the boundaries of its home town, Croydon.

Locally, it is hard to imagine a home that doesn't have a piece of furniture bought from E. Reeves. So well-known is the business that when the road system in the area was redrawn in 1977, Reeves' Corner took over from Church Street as its official postal address.

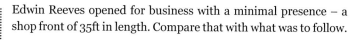

The present chief executives, Trevor and Graham Reeves, are the great great grandsons of the founder of the company, Edwin Reeves.

It was in 1867 when Edwin Reeves arrived in Croydon from Sherborne, Dorset. Queen Victoria was mid-way through her reign, the Crimean War was over, the American Civil War had concluded and the Industrial Revolution was at its height.

Edwin Reeves opened for business with a minimal presence – a shop front of 35ft in length. Compare that with what was to follow.

Edwin's trade was as a cooper and barrel maker and that's how he started in business in Croydon. But helped by his wife and brother, he soon branched out into other areas. Ironmongery, for example, became one of the first new skills to be added.

Before too much longer what was to become the famous Reeves' connection with furniture was made. As demand grew it was one of his four sons, William Arthur, who helped the business expand

Left: Church Street, since renamed Reeves' Corner. Above: The founder of the company, Edwin Reeves in the stove pipe hat.

Above: Reeves opened branches in Sherborne (left) and Caterham (right) which both helped the business to grow.

and ultimately he took charge in 1913. Ye Old Curiosite Shoppe, as it was known, took over several neighbouring properties during the First World War and by 1917 an auction room had been added along with showrooms for second hand furniture.

The business went from strength to strength and more branches were opened, one of them in Sherborne, the town where William Arthur's father had come from 50 years earlier. Two more sites, one in Croydon and another in Caterham, presented the opportunity to sell timber and building materials so widening the scope of the business.

The first auctions were held at Church Street in 1917 and by November, 1937, exactly 1,000 had been held. The onset of World War Two meant that all manufacturing had to be devoted to the war effort so good quality second hand furniture was in huge demand and Reeves helped to meet it.

In 1947, the firm became E. Reeves Ltd and William Arthur's son, William Thomas, its managing director. William Thomas carried

on at the helm until he passed away at the age of 82. William Thomas was succeeded by his son, Maurice, the father of Trevor and Graham. The three of them have strong sporting connections in the area. Maurice was a cricketer of some note while Graham was an excellent golfer. Maurice's interest in motor sport was inherited by Trevor who was a rallycross and circuit racing champion.

E. Reeves Ltd went on to concentrate on the sale of new furniture. Holding a vast range of stock it can supply most customers' requirements immediately, a refreshing change from some retailers who keep customers waiting for weeks.

It is this kind of efficiency and determination to succeed that over the years has seen House of Reeves, as it is now known, overcome the kind of setback that would have killed off lesser firms.

The business came to worldwide public attention following rioting in London in August, 2011. The images beamed around the world of the furniture store going up in flames following an arson attack

Above and right: Reeves delivery vans from the 60s and 20s in front of the same building.

Above: The island site before the fire. *Left:* The arson attack in 2011.

became a symbol of steadfast family values in complete contrast to the behaviour of the perpetrators of the events that spread across the country. The rioting affected 50,000 retailers and more than 40 town centres were attacked.

Following the destruction of the store on Reeves Corner, Maurice Reeves, 80 at that time, came out of retirement to be the figurehead for the massive media attention which followed, allowing the rest of the family and staff to clear up and rebuild the business and the running of the furniture store alongside his sons, Trevor and Graham.

House of Reeves has seen many changes in its long and proud history battling through two world wars and the depressions of the 1930s and, more recently, the 1970s and 2007 recessions.

As a close family, Maurice and his sons were convinced that they could rebuild the destroyed store and continue trading. Although fraught with difficulties, plans to rebuild on the original site may happen in the future.

Above: The decorative hoarding charting the Reeves family history.

After the initial shock of dealing with the aftermath of the fire, Croydon and the wider community got behind the Reeves' family.

"The passionate support from all over the world was overwhelming," said Trevor Reeves. "It gave us the confidence and resourcefulness to revitalise old storage areas and create a new furniture showroom to continue trading with the minimum reduction in selling area.

Left: The island site in 2016.

Above: How Reeves marked the first anniversary of the fire.

"The local community support forms the main basis for our recent, more committed, attitude towards the positive development of our community and the future of its young people.

"Once the fired building was demolished we placed a decorative hoarding around the Reeves Corner site which featured many images of our history.

Above: Part of the gabled and oval chimney architecture destroyed in 2011.

"This pictorial view of the family, the area and its history stimulated a much needed respect and realisation that there was, indeed, a great history, not only at Reeves but the whole of Old Town Croydon, that had been forgotten and needed preservation".

"Continuing the theme of young people, the first anniversary of the fire was marked by the remaining building being covered in small pictoral messages, all from young people, with captions of good deeds and achievement. A complete reversal of the attitude that caused the destruction in the first place.

Almost six years on from the riots, House of Reeves is thriving again. "That is down to the hard work of the staff and support we have received from the community for our revitalised store at Reeves Corner," said Mr Reeves "We are looking to the future and the continued progression and rejuvenation of the Reeves Corner area.

Mr Reeves said the engagement of local people had kept the business afloat. "We felt we owed it to them to reciprocate so we joined the Citizen UK campaign promoting retail stores as safe havens for young people who feel intimidated and in danger when they are on the streets.

"We have received requests from local schools for information about the riots, how Citizenship works and what it is like running a business. I like to think that we have taken time and made every effort to respond to all the requests. We hope that our efforts will help give something back to the communities that supported us so strongly at a time when we needed it most.

"Where the business is concerned we aim to carry on the traditions of past generations for years to come and look forward to Croydon's long overdue revitalisation".

Rowland Brothers
Coping with the darkest days

Losing someone you love is one of life's most difficult experiences.

It is a deeply distressing time and while grief, quite naturally, is the overriding emotion there are seemingly endless practical issues to consider.

Rowland Brothers is a family owned and run firm of funeral directors that has helped bereaved families in the Croydon and South London area since 1873.

A funeral can involve a lot of complicated decision-making and paperwork - at a time when the bereaved are potentially least able to cope. But Rowland Brothers have decades of experience to place at their disposal to ensure that all their wishes, and those of the deceased, are carried out to the letter.

In addition to the big decisions about cremation or burial, religious or civil ceremony and the choice of venue, there are a number of important details to cope with.

Its staff believes they have an important role in caring for family members, not just by providing support in the days leading up to the funeral, but especially through the difficult days that lie ahead.

They appreciate that the bereaved are going through a variety of emotions and will do all they can to help guide them through.

"We pride ourselves on providing our clients with a personal and attentive service of the highest standard," says Chairman Tony Rowland.

"For whatever reason they require our help they can be assured of our best attention at all times. That applies whether they are newly bereaved, struggling with grief issues or looking for ways to help a family member, a friend or a colleague."

Balancing practicalities with sympathy is something that can only come with experience and Rowland Brothers has more than 140 years of conducting funerals and caring for the bereaved on which to draw. Managing bereavement with dignity is the way the firm has operated since William and Harry Rowland established the business in 1873.

Initially, William was more involved in the building trade than

Above: Harry Rowland leads the cortege at the last horse-drawn funeral.

with undertaking but soon after the First World War the emphasis changed and the demand for funeral directors grew rapidly.

By the end of the 20th century the firm had developed into an international concern, as ready to deal with bereavements on the other side of the world as it is to handle those in its surrounding area.

The firm's headquarters in Whitehorse Road, Croydon, have been the base for five generations of the Rowland family. Now the premises comprise several houses which are used for offices and living accommodation. There are large workshops where coffins and memorials are prepared.

A garage complex houses the fleet of hearses and limousines along with private ambulances for local, national, and international collections.

A chapel of remembrance where the bereaved can spend time with their loved one was built in 1953 and a new chapel complex housing seven chapels catering for all religions was added in 1985.

While the business has moved forward the values William Rowland instilled into his four sons comfortingly remain much the same.

The last surviving son, Harry, continued to run the business until the premises suffered bomb damage in 1943.

Arthur's wife, Muriel, ran the company from its patched up offices until 1945. Muriel, at the age of 98, is still coming into the office for three days a week. Harry's two sons, Arthur and James, returned from serving in North Africa and Normandy and set about the task of rebuilding the business.

The premises were little more than a shed and a few other outbuildings. There were no tools and wood lay rotting among the rubble. The only option was to rebuild and this they did, the phoenix rising from the ashes.

Arthur's sons, Tony, David and Bob, took over and continued to build and expand the business until it became one of the most prominent funeral directors in the Croydon area.

They were joined by Tony's wife, Margaret, and David's wife, Janet. Tony's children, Melanie and Stephen, became the

Above: Three generations of the family pictured in 1994. Below: Muriel Rowland at work in 2009. She still comes into the office three days a week at the age of 98.

next generation of the family to play an active role. They joined in 1983 and 1990 respectively. Muriel's brother Michael Reed also joined the team and David's son, Andrew, joined the business in 1997 to form a true family concern. Ben and Joe Walkling, Melanie's sons are the latest generation to join the company and they look forward to ensuring that Rowland Brothers' continues as a family business. Rowland Brothers is probably unique in Croydon if not the country as its boasts four generations of the same family working in the business.

In 1971, Tony extended the business under the name of Rowland Brothers International whose influence quickly spread across the globe providing a repatriation service to British tourists who pass away abroad. Now there is a Rowland's agent in almost every town, city and country.

Distance is no object and the Rowland Brothers chain of contacts ensures an efficient and caring service at all times.

It takes experience and inside knowledge to be able to cut through the red tape that exists in many countries. As well as dealing sympathetically with grieving relatives, often separated from their loved ones, there is a mountain of bureaucracy to tackle.

One of the more challenging areas of repatriation is dealing with the customs and practices of another faith or culture. Rowland's

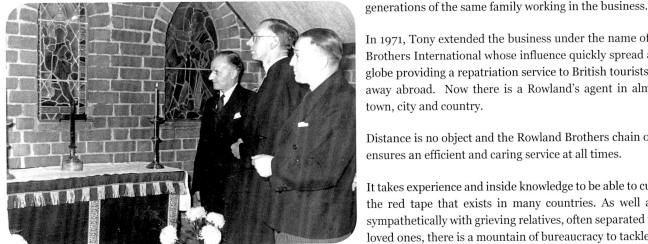

Above: Arthur and Jim Rowland watch the blessing of the chapel at Whitehorse Road in 1957 by the Rev. Canon Ingram of Canterbury Cathedral.

staff has been fully trained to respect the beliefs of all faiths and act accordingly.

Through their international contacts the firm has access to the quality furnishings from around the world that place them at the forefront of the funeral directing business.

Meanwhile, David and Bob Rowland developed the monumental masons' division which has been awarded several commissions including the Kenley war memorial at Kenley Aerodrome, the Help for Heroes memorial at Headley Court and the memorial for C.W. Alcock, creator of the FA Cup. They also developed what at the time was a new service – grave maintenance plans to ensure that families' graves were cleaned and had flowers placed on them to mark special anniversaries.

Left: *Rowland Brothers repatriation service uses the latest transportation methods.*

Rowland Brothers, which has other branches in Purley, Coulsdon, Warlingham and New Addington can claim that it provides more than just a funeral service by offering a pre-paid plan to meet funeral expenses. It was one of the first companies in the UK to do this.

'Golden Leaves' was established in 1984 by Tony Rowland whose son, Stephen, further developed the scheme into a company providing funeral plans throughout the UK and Europe to British Expatriates living abroad.

More than simply funeral directors, Rowland Brothers reach out into the community providing a comprehensive bereavement support service, where assistance is given to those left on their own after the loss of a partner. Help might be a simple matter such as advising how to write cheque or change an electrical plug, cook a simple meal or feed the electricity meter. Counselling can be arranged with in-depth advice on coping with loss. They provide monthly working groups for the bereaved to attend within their local communities bringing together bereaved people to talk through their experiences and how they have coped.

Annual seminars and workshops are provided for those professionals who come into contact with the bereaved such as nursing home staff, doctors ministers and MacMillan nurses.

When the Purley branch was opened in 1995 a special fortnight was arranged when local community carers were given the opportunity to meet with members of the public and deal with delicate subjects such as cot death and social security benefits to help with expenses. There was also guidance from Age Concern,

Above and right: *The Help For Heroes memorial tribute at Hedley Court and the war memorial at Kenley Aerodrome – both constructed by Rowland Brothers.*

the Terence Higgins Trust and investment groups.

In this and many other ways the after care service is one of the most important features of Rowland's comprehensive service.

"We want to help organise a funeral that lets you remember your loved one with dignity and with respect," says Tony. "We believe that the funeral is a vital part of coming to terms with a bereavement and that, accordingly, the day should be as memorable and meaningful as possible.

"But we also understand that organising the funeral and dealing with the red tape can sometimes be distressing. That's why, at the time you may need it most, we're here to offer support, guidance, care and reassurance every step of the way."

From humble beginnings Rowland Brothers has become an integral part of the communities they serve. They are considered the company to go to and have been privileged to provide funeral services for five ex-mayors of Croydon, local councillors and a number of high profile people such as Kirsty MacColl - whose coffin was carried by members of the band U2 - and the 5th Lord Mostyn of Llandudno. Repatriation and funeral services were provided in the tragic case of Meredith Kercher; the repatriation of David Cameron's father and all 157 British casualties in the Boxing Day Tsunami in Indonesia in 2004.

Above: A police force funeral at Croydon Minster. *Below:* Tony Rowland conducts a Masonic funeral at the Minster.

Above: The partners pictured in 2011: From left, Steve Rowland, Melanie Walkling and Tony Rowland. Melanie sadly died in 2012.

Boyden and Co Ltd
Selecting tiles with style

It was a happy accident that led to Boyden and Co setting up – and becoming hugely successful – in the ceramics business.

The company, originally importers of Japanese silk, had placed a substantial order for the material but when the consignment arrived and the containers were opened they were found to contain ceramic tiles.

The decision had to be made to either sell the tiles or run the risk of the business folding. The rest – as they say – is history. The company has been importing and distributing ceramic tiles for more than 90 years and is the largest stockist in London and the south east.

Boyden's, named after the founder's secretary and friend, Rose Boyden, is one of the best-known names within the industry and is a true family business. It has a proud history and is still wholly owned and managed by the Frei family, now in its third generation.

The company operates from a distribution centre in Mayday Road, Croydon, and has showrooms in Epsom, Sutton and Purley Way.

The showrooms attract many retail customers because of the way in which the large number of ranges in stock are presented in stunning displays and settings. The showrooms also act as a shop window for tiling contractors and independent businesses which rely on Boyden's for their supplies.

Kitchen and bathroom showrooms requiring imaginative co-ordinating tiles also rely on Boyden's because of its exceptional service and competitive prices.

Above: The founder, John Frei (centre) with factory managers at Johnson Tiles, Stoke.

With expert advice from knowledgeable staff in the showrooms and customer services centre technical help is only a phone call away.

Deliveries for most orders are free within an 80-mile radius of the Croydon depot and carried out the next working day unless otherwise requested by the customer. The company also has a large internet presence under its 'tileexperience' brand.

Major projects completed by Boyden's include The Shard, London Underground, St Pancras Eurostar Terminal and Heathrow Terminal 5.

Boyden's currently employs approximately 50 staff with six of them having over 25 years of loyal service. The company is proud to have been based in the Croydon area for most of its history providing local jobs and a range of benefits for the local community.

Left: Boyden's display at the '100 Years of Croydon' exhibition in 1960. Below: Boyden's shop in Gloucester Road in 1960.

Rawlings Opticians
Helping Croydon "get better looking" for over 120 years

If you are struggling to read this then you are not alone. Some 60 per cent of the population wear glasses or contact lenses.

Rawlings has been offering its clients excellent eyecare and eyewear in, and around Croydon for over 120 years.

The experienced and highly qualified staff help customers choose the best solutions for their unique visual demands - as well as their pockets. That way satisfaction is guaranteed as value for money is not found in just the cost of the frame.

The personal touch and after sales service by qualified Dispensing Opticians are difficult to measure but are an invaluable part of what has allowed Rawlings to remain at the forefront of optics for over a century.

The family firm, which goes back four generations, began life at North End, Croydon, in 1895.

Alfred J. Rawling opened his shop as a combination of the jewellery, watchmaking and optical trades. As a child, times had been hard. It was no fun in the Victorian era to be one of five children brought up by a widowed mother. It gave Alfred a determination to succeed and make his own mark on life.

He was still in his 20s when he banked his first day's takings – the princely sum of six shillings (30p).

Although apprenticed to his uncle as a jeweller and watchmaker, it was in the optical side of his own business that he showed a special interest.

While still working in the shop he trained as an optician and passed the examinations of the Worshipful Company of Spectacle Makers in 1904. The diploma still has pride of place on the wall at Rawlings Opticians on Brighton Road, Purley.

The back rooms of the shop were used as consulting rooms while an assistant ran the other business interests from the front.

His wife, Hilda, gave birth to five children. The four boys all became Ophthalmic Opticians and daughter, Ruth, was book keeper for 30 years.

The business expanded and successive generations have all been involved in this growth. Branches opened in Purley, Caterham, Winchester and Alton to name but a few.

By the time the 21st century came around eight Rawlings Opticians, as the business is now known, can be found.

Top: *Founder of the business, Alfred Rawling.* ***Left:*** *The original shop in the early years of the 20th century.*

ACKNOWLEDGMENTS

The publisher would like to sincerely thank the following individuals and organisations for their help and contribution to this publication:

Local Studies Croydon Library

Mirrorpix

David Bradley
(www.trolleybus.net)

Getty Images

John Spring & Fairfield Halls
(www.fairfield.co.uk)

Wikimedia Commons